Inside the Disney Marketing Machine

Other Books by Lorraine Santoli

The Top Ten Secrets to Organizing a Nonfiction Book (2013)
Disneyland Resort: Magical Memories for a Lifetime (2002)
The Official Mickey Mouse Club Book (1995)

Inside the Disney Marketing Machine

In the Era of
Michael Eisner and Frank Wells

Lorraine Santoli

Theme Park Press
www.ThemeParkPress.com

Editor: Bob McLain
Layout: Artisanal Text

ISBN 978-1-941500-48-4
Printed in the United States of America

Theme Park Press | www.ThemeParkPress.com
Address queries to bob@themeparkpress.com

*This book is dedicated to Gail Brown,
friend and colleague who exemplified what
it meant to be a Disney cast member.
She left this earth too soon.*

Contents

Foreword

I was Lorraine Santoli's first boss and mentor. I am honored that she asked me to write the foreword to this book, not only because we met at the beginning of her career and have remained friends for so many years, but because I feel my experience as a former NBC-TV Marketing, Research, and Strategic Planning executive qualifies me to say that *Inside the Disney Marketing Machine: In the Era of Michael Eisner and Frank Wells* is an important business book.

It was 1968. I was manager of Marketing and Management Studies in the NBC Research Department. Since NBC was owned at that time by RCA, our office was located in NBC's corporate headquarters in the RCA Building in Rockefeller Center in midtown Manhattan. We had a prestigious address: 30 Rockefeller Plaza—made famous now by the TV series 30 Rock.

My main job was to develop new ways to segment network television audiences for advertisers beyond the standard Nielsen ratings—in particular, by the product and brand usage characteristics of these audiences. While most people probably believe that NBC's product is its programming, in point of fact its product is the audience its programming garners. The audience is then marketed to advertisers and their agencies.

I had arrived at NBC four years earlier after working for several years at arguably the most iconic advertising agency of that "Mad Men" era: Doyle Dane Bernbach. Just as Michael Eisner and Frank Wells were a perfect fit in their era of running The Walt Disney Company, the same was true at DDB: Ned Doyle ran account management, Maxwell Dane supervised the business side, and Bill Bernbach was the creative genius. My more humble job in DDB's Research Department was to supervise strategic marketing research for the agency's fast-growing and diverse roster of clients, which included Volkswagen, Polaroid, and American Airlines. Our analysis of one client, Avis Rent-A-Car, led to the development of their famous slogan, "We're #2/We Try Harder".

While working at Doyle Dane Bernbach, I also earned a Ph.D. in Economics at New York University. Shortly after obtaining my Ph.D., I secured the position in the NBC Research Department that I described previously. Against this background, in 1968 I needed a new secretary and interviewed several applicants—one of whom was Lorraine Santoli. She was barely out of her teens at that time. I don't remember the interview now. But inasmuch as I hired her, I obviously was impressed by her and liked her as a person.

Who could have predicted back then that Lorraine over the next few decades would not only advance from secretary at NBC to corporate director at Disney, but, more importantly, that she would play a key role in developing a major new tool of marketing management: internal corporate marketing? Who knew?

I stayed at NBC for most of the remainder of my business career, moving on to become director of Research Projects and a few years later assuming the role of director of Economic Planning. I eventually retired from NBC after 25 years of service, then worked for a few years in investment banking, and finally packed it in permanently.

After Lorraine left NBC, moved to California, and began working at Disney, we kept in touch, and I followed with pleasure her advancing career. Then, when I fully retired, my wife, Cynthia, and I decided to move to southern California ourselves. We ended up residing not far from Lorraine's location and became good personal friends. My connection with her had moved full circle.

Why This Is a Must-Read Business Book

As I said in the opening of this foreword, Lorraine Santoli's *Inside the Disney Marketing Machine: In the Era of Michael Eisner and Frank Wells* is an important business book.

Primarily, this book provides a unique behind-the-scenes account of how The Walt Disney Company marketed its properties not only outside the company to consumers (Part One: Marketing Outside the Company), but in the mid-1980s launching and implementing an internal marketing program (Part Two: Marketing Inside the Company).

While Marketing Outside the Company provides significant insight into Disney's approach, Marketing Inside the Company, was indeed unique to the Disney company during the Eisner and Wells years. The purpose of this program was to keep all divisions and business units of the vast Disney organization informed about what was going on around the company, and more importantly, to motivate cross-promotion of what they were all doing. The ultimate goal was to achieve *synergy*, where the sum of all these interactions by different divisions (in revenues and profits) would be greater than each division could achieve on its own. As Michael Eisner succinctly put it, with synergy "1+1=3".

A prerequisite but no guarantee for achieving synergy within any large corporation is the support of top management. Certainly, Disney's effort at attaining synergy had the full and enthusiastic support of CEO Michael Eisner and his able partner, Frank Wells, who was president and chief operating officer.

A Corporate Synergy Department, where Lorraine worked as a manager and then director, was set up to implement the synergy program. This entailed recruiting synergy representatives from all areas of Disney, developing databases of these contacts, creating a slate of internal communications, distributing calendars, building relationships across business segments, and more, to keep all marketing and key company executives aware of ongoing business activities throughout the company. She also set up working groups at different levels of management, and scheduled frequent meetings and events where participants could bond with each other. In the mid-1990s, when the internet was still in its infancy, Disney's Corporate Synergy Department actually launched an intranet to communicate with synergy representatives. Nearly 1,000 Disney marketing, entertainment, and creative executives were in the synergy loop.

The challenging task that Disney's Corporate Synergy Department faced was to motivate people around the company to get on the synergy bandwagon, when they of course did not report to Corporate Synergy. (This will increasingly become the norm in American business and industry, as organizational structures flatten and hierarchical chains-of-command disappear. Successful managers will have to lead teams of people who don't report to them. Motivational and collegial skills—building relationships —will be the key to success.)

Lorraine discovered unusual ways to motivate her synergy contacts, one of which was through food. She had regular 9 am breakfast synergy meetings. Before the meetings food would be available—but not just the usual coffee and Danish pastries. She arranged lavish buffets of bagels and lox, juices, muffins, cereals, etc. Not surprisingly, everybody got to the meetings early and had a chance to bond with each other. They were also in a very good mood (although perhaps a couple of pounds heavier) when the meetings started. (This is the kind of practical lesson that you are not likely to learn at even the most advanced marketing seminar at the Harvard Business School.)

How much did the synergy program contribute to Disney's bottom-line during the Eisner/Wells era (1984-1994)? This was a golden period when everything seemed to be going right for the company, and they made enormous amounts of money. Probably, quite substantial shares of the growth in revenues and profits can be attributed to the synergy program.

More important, perhaps, than monetary gains, the synergy program fostered teamwork and the bonding of people across the many business units of Disney.

Final Thoughts

Lorraine Santoli's achievements are especially remarkable when you realize that she entered the business world in 1968. While opportunities were beginning to open up for women—especially in industries like advertising, media, and entertainment—it was not likely that a woman who started her career as a secretary would get much farther up the ladder. Almost invariably, women in the same jobs as men were paid less. Barriers to entry and advancement also blocked people from minority groups and with different sexual orientations.

It is painful now to think of how many bright, creative, and talented people with great potential never had the opportunity to realize that potential—and what a waste that was for American business and the entire economy.

In today's increasingly competitive global economy—and with disruptive new technologies and business models shaking up established industries—companies need every competitive advantage they can get. We can no longer afford to squander what economists call our "human capital".

I've discussed previously the flattening of corporate organizational structures, where successful managers will be working with teams of people who don't report to them. Motivational, relationship-building skills will be the key to personal and business success. Women, in particular, are apt to have these needed skills. It is more vital than ever that they have the opportunity to realize their full potential. Lorraine rose to the occasion, and with her book *Inside the Disney Marketing Machine: In the Era of Michael Eisner and Frank Wells*, shares a marketing wisdom that should be required reading for marketers everywhere.

Sam Tuchman, Ph.D.
June 2015

Introduction

For years I've heard from people who wonder what it was like to be employed by The Walt Disney Company, especially from a marketing perspective since the organization has always been lauded for its genius in that discipline. Having worked inside the Disney marketing machine for over two decades, from 1978 to 2000, I decided to share my experiences through this book. It is part memoir, part "take-a-lesson", and will provide a peek into what goes on behind the marketing doors of the Mouse House, specifically during my tenure.

Marketing is defined by the American Marketing Association as the activity, set of institutions, and processes for creating, communicating, delivering, and exchanging offerings that have value for customers, clients, partners, and society at large. It is an umbrella term under which advertising, publicity and promotions reside. My perspective in writing this book is derived from my personal experiences working in marketing positions both at The Walt Disney Studios in Burbank, California (home of Disney filmmaking and the global headquarters for The Walt Disney Company) and at the Disneyland Resort in Anaheim, California.

My Disney adventure started back in February 1978 when I relocated from New York City to Los Angeles on a whim after a decade-long career at NBC where I was headquartered at 30 Rock, an address quite well known today from the TV series of the same name. There, I worked my way up from secretary to Sam Tuchman, Ph.D., a TV research analysis executive (and my first mentor), to media analyst to camera person, becoming a crew member on such TV shows as *The Today Show*, *Saturday Night Live*, and an early Barbara Walters syndicated talk show called *Not For Women Only*.

But I was ready for a new adventure. I wanted to write for television, and Los Angeles was my target. Fortunately, I had an NBC co-worker, my good friend Suzy Hey, who was also ready for a change, so we packed up my car and headed west. Neither of us knew a soul in California. What we did know was that we both needed to get a job as quickly as possible once we arrived.

We settled in what was then the sleepy town of Burbank, renting a beautiful two-bedroom furnished apartment with a full spectrum of amenities including a pool, tennis courts, and game rooms. Having been born and bred in Brooklyn, New York, it was like I died and went to heaven. But to maintain my new L.A. lifestyle, job hunting was a number one priority.

Two weeks into my arrival I was well into applying for jobs all over town, mostly at TV stations. Then one day I came upon The Walt Disney Studios, also located in Burbank. Who knew? The only clue that this was Disney was a small sign affixed to chain link fence at the entry that read: Walt Disney Productions (the name was changed to The Walt Disney Company in 1986). Might as well put in an application there, too, I thought. I was hired that day.

Like most everyone, I grew up with Disney. I faithfully watched the *Mickey Mouse Club* as a child and I wanted to be a Mouseketeer. I was glued to the TV screen watching the weekly *Disneyland* show, especially enjoying Walt Disney's glimpses into a new entertainment complex he was building in Anaheim, California, called Disneyland. And, of course, I enjoyed Disney animated and live-action films. While I was a Disney kid, I never specifically had my sights set on working for the company. But here I was, having been hired as an assistant in the market research area of the Publicity Department. I knew little about marketing, but what an education was ahead.

My tenure at Disney would span 22 years. In my journey, I first served as an assistant in the Publicity Department at The Walt Disney Studios, moved up to become a publicist in TV and Film Publicity, relocated to the Disneyland Resort as supervisor of Publicity and returned to the studio as manager of Corporate Marketing and finally director of Corporate Synergy in my final decade with the company. I lived deep inside the Disney marketing machine from day one to my final exit.

Part One of this book, "Marketing Outside the Company", explores my early forays into that specialty for several years before Michael Eisner and Frank Wells took over the Disney reins. The book then moves forward with a deep dive into a new world of hyper-marketing when they came on board.

Part Two, "Marketing Inside the Company", shines a light on the amazing revitalization of the Disney Company under the leadership of Eisner and Wells. The story will focus on how they brought a new energy to Disney marketing by incorporating a company-wide synergy strategy to make the most of every corporate asset. Synergy, of course, underscored an organizational "working together" mindset that would cross-divisional lines and eradicate silo-based thinking. It was a concept that was initiated by Walt Disney many decades ago.

From 1990 to 2000 I occupied the heart of the Disney synergy machine as director of Corporate Synergy. How the synergy team so successfully fostered that concept throughout the company, an often-asked question, will be brought to the forefront. Read carefully, it works!

Michael Eisner once explained, "We insisted that each division help the other fellow. For the Disney Company, 'help the other fellow' meant the movie division would create a film...that could become a theme park ride or attraction...that could become a consumer product...that could become a television show...that could become a film sequel...that could become a cable show...that could become an international attraction...that could become a musical on Broadway...it goes on and on. But to accomplish that, everybody had to cooperate with each other, with no place for jealousy, and no competition between divisions. That's an unlikely reality in corporate America. But at Disney, we worked things differently."

Indeed we did.

And, at that time, we did so without the power of the technology that exists today. We were not yet living in a digital world; we were just getting used to utilizing computers and mobile phones. Today, the masses believe that we need to know everything about everybody, and we need to know it right now. Social media websites are the binoculars through which we peer into people's daily lives. Facebook, LinkedIn, Twitter, YouTube, Pinterest, Instagram, and others provide the landscape for sharing even the most intimate details of one's life. But while the social arena thrives on connection, the business environment, where collaboration and information sharing is vital to profitability, is often not optimized. It's like leaving money on the floor.

On social media platforms, people now let it all hang out. Perhaps it's an ego inflator, the ultimate selfie or an emphatic shout-out to others to "notice me!" In any case, we can easily find out where our friends are at any given moment, learn what they like to eat and where they like to eat it, what their favorite TV shows are, the kind of music they listen to, how many times their baby cried last night, what they thought about a new movie, and everything else that anyone cares to discuss.

The digital devices we use to get connected—mobile phones, computers, tablets, and now even wrist watches—make it all possible at lightning speed whether through the use of email and texting, or visually through photos and video. It's instantaneous communication all the time. Is there an advantage to being connected 24/7? From a social perspective having hundreds of friends worldwide can be informative and entertaining, although one must always be mindful of the internet's darker side and tread carefully. However, if you need a new car, you can just poll your friends and get feedback; if you need a recommendation for a good plumber, you just need to put the word out; or if you're seeking a new pet, just ask.

Michael Eisner and Frank Wells knew that communication and connection were the keys to elevating the Disney Company to a new level. They led a synergy charge that brought explosive growth, phenomenal success, and skyrocketing profits to Disney. Incorporating synergy into every corner of the corporation played a significant role in reaching those heights. In doing so, the Disney Company became a well-oiled marketing machine where no stone remained unturned when it came to fostering internal cross-promotion on priority projects.

In the process of writing *Inside the Disney Marketing Machine*, I had the opportunity to interview many former and current Disney executives with whom I worked during my time at the company. Although I have shined a light on those colleagues, certainly many, many more were instrumental in Disney's success. We were all a team.

Today the Disney Company is the number one entertainment company in the world, employing vastly different strategies, tactics, and marketing approaches to energize the organization. The synergy processes and programs put into place during my tenure at the company, and described in this book, have long since been changed, and rightfully so, with current top management having successfully guided the organization into the 21st century.

In that regard my book is written from a historical perspective, covering marketing milestones during the tenure of the "dream team" of Michael Eisner and Frank Wells. It was a special moment in time when all the stars seemed to be perfectly aligned and everything turned to gold.

Marketing then was, in Disney jargon, an "E" ticket. (The phrase "E ticket" refers to the admission ticket system used at Disney theme parks before 1982 where the "E" ticket admitted the bearer to the newest and most advanced rides.)

Eisner and Wells charted a new course that reawakened and renewed the sleeping giant that was The Walt Disney Company in the mid-1980s and 1990s. That's what this book is about. I hope you enjoy the ride.

Lorraine Santoli
June 2015

PART ONE

Marketing Outside the Company

CHAPTER ONE

Hello, Disney!

It was late February 1978 when I first set foot on the lot of The Walt Disney Studios. Back home in New York the weather was brutally cold, but here I was in the warm sunshine of Burbank, California, starting a new job and a new life.

The world in 1978 was a lot different than the world of today. Jimmy Carter was president, the top movies were *Grease*, *Close Encounters of the Third Kind*, *Saturday Night Fever*, and *The Deer Hunter*. It was the year we saw the introduction of the first-ever cellular mobile phone system, and *Happy Days*, *Charlie's Angels*, and *The Love Boat* were the most popular shows on TV.

At Disney, three films were released in that year—*Return from Witch Mountain*, *The Cat from Outer Space*, and *Hot Lead and Cold Feet*. Not exactly blockbusters. *The Wonderful World of Disney* weekly TV series was also in production at the studio. E. Cardon Walker, a long-time Disney executive, was CEO of Walt Disney Productions, and Ron Miller, Walt Disney's son-in-law (married to Walt's daughter, Diane Disney), was president of the company. Walker retired in 1983 and Miller was upped to CEO, but his tenure lasted just a year until 1984. It was then that Eisner and Wells arrived on the scene and big changes were in the wind.

But in 1978, the studio was a small player among the Hollywood elite. It was, however, an enviable workplace with its well-manicured green lawns, towering trees, and flowering bushes that lined Mickey Avenue, its main thoroughfare. One side of Mickey Avenue housed the studio Post Office (with its Mickey Mouse mailbox out front), The Walt Disney Studios commissary (with outdoor dining patio), and the R.O.D. (Roy O. Disney) Building, where my new office was located.

On the other side of the street stood the Casting Building, the Orchestra Stage, and the Animation Building. Making a turn at the intersection of Mickey Avenue and Dopey Drive, you'd find a full-sized movie theater across from the entrance to the Animation Building. Park benches dotted the landscape that also served as home to the friendliest squirrels in

Burbank. It looked very much like a college campus (so much so that many times it stood in for "Medfield College" in numerous Disney live-action film comedies). The studio had come a long way from its humble beginnings.

The Disney Bros. Cartoon Studio was started in the summer of 1923 in the Los Angeles garage of Robert Disney (Walt's uncle), and later moved to a self-built studio on Hyperion Avenue in the city's Silver Lake district just a few miles from downtown Los Angeles. After fourteen years, and much success with the creation of Mickey Mouse in 1928 and the release of *Snow White and the Seven Dwarfs*, the world's first feature-length animated film, in 1937, the company had expanded to a degree that Walt and his brother and partner, Roy, agreed that they needed to build an all-new, studio plant.

In 1939, they paid $100,000 for a 51-acre site on Buena Vista Street in Burbank, just over the hills of Griffith Park, for the purpose of developing a modern studio specifically designed for making animated films. All parts of the new studio were custom designed in accordance with the wishes of the Disney brothers working with architect and industrial designer Kem Weber. Specially designed features included furniture, landscape, roads, recreational spaces, and the buildings themselves.

A large Animation Building was set in the center of the campus, with adjacent buildings for the Story Department, the Music Department, the Ink & Paint Department, and the other various functions of the studio. Both aboveground walkways and underground tunnels connected many of the buildings.

In the late 1940s, the studio also began regular work on live-action features, and although their first films were shot in England, the necessity to build live-action facilities arose. Lacking the capital to do it themselves, in the 1950s actor and producer Jack Webb offered to put up some of the money to build live-action stages in exchange for his being able to use one of the stages to shoot much of his *Dragnet* TV series. During this time, a back lot with various exterior sets was also built and remained standing at the studio until the management change of the mid-1980s with Eisner and Wells. The old back lot area was re-modeled to accommodate more live-action production space and administrative offices.

Today, the studio lot is made up of multiple office and administration buildings and ten soundstages. However, back in 1978 when I arrived, I still had the opportunity to enjoy many strolls on the old back lot. I often had the opportunity of eating my lunch in various locales, such as the Western street where family-friendly Disney cowboy movies were shot, the outdoor *Zorro* El Pueblo de los Angeles set, and an old-fashioned swing set in front of a Victorian home façade on the suburban "neighborhood" street. It was fun just to take a leisurely walk around the "anytown" Town Square location where so many Disney films and TV shows were shot.

After working in the hustle, bustle, and high-rises of midtown Manhattan for a decade, residing and having my workplace in small town Burbank at the then leisurely paced Disney Studio just a few miles northeast of Hollywood was quite a change.

In 1978, Burbank was a city with a population of about 85,000. It is today billed as the "Media Capital of the World" because of the entertainment companies that are headquartered or have significant production facilities there. In addition to Disney, Burbank is home to Warner Bros. Entertainment, Warner Music Group, ABC, The Cartoon Network, Nickelodeon, Cookie Jar Entertainment, New Wave Entertainment, and NBCUniversal. In fact it was NBC that made the city famous with the references to "Beautiful Downtown Burbank" on the TV shows *Laugh-In* and *The Tonight Show Starring Johnny Carson*.

The average cost of a new house in 1978 was $54,800, the median income was $17,000, monthly rent averaged $260, the Dow Jones was just over 800, and the cost of a gallon of gas was 63 cents! But remember, average salaries were commensurate with those numbers, too. Still, it surely felt like life was good.

I soon settled into my Disney position as assistant to Martin Rabinovitch, Ph.D., who handled research analysis in conjunction with Disney's upcoming slate of films. Martin oversaw testing of print ads, trailers (movie "coming attractions"), TV and radio commercials, etc., to determine those that inspired the most consumer interest in seeing the film.

In the process, he designed questionnaires, led focus groups and worked within the marketing arena of advertising, publicity, and promotions on a day-to-day basis to optimize Disney film campaigns. I loved working with Martin, but I also paid close attention to everything that was going on around me. In fact, before long it was what was going on around me that really fueled my upward ambitions.

Martin's office was located smack-dab in the middle of the Publicity Department on the 3rd floor of the R.O.D. Building. I had a front row seat to what was going on with that aspect of marketing and I loved it. As a kid, I had collected autographs and still have my collection of about 400 prominent celebrity signatures. I spent many, many hours hanging around stage doors at Broadway theaters, in the lobby of NBC's 30 Rock where so many variety and game shows were videotaped (and where I got my first job), and at the Ed Sullivan Theater where rehearsals took place every weekend for Sullivan's Sunday night show.

Now, here I was watching a staff of publicists interact daily with celebrities, interviewing them, setting up lunches for them with media and attending those lunches themselves to guide the conversation, traveling to movie locations, spending time on soundstages during production, setting up photo shoots, and writing stories about the films and TV shows they were working on. Writing! That's why I headed to California in the first place. And although it wasn't writing for TV, which had been my career goal, writing as a publicist and performing all the tasks mentioned above looked like a lot more fun.

After putting in just over a year working as an assistant in market research, I was able to graduate to the trailer department writing the text for coming attractions for several Disney films including the re-release of *Bambi*. It was fun and a great learning experience, but not my ultimate goal of becoming a publicist. Then I started helping one of the young publicists, Michael Russell, who oversaw TV publicity. He was a one-man-band in that arena, and needed assistance with his workload, particularly for the weekly *Wonderful World of Disney* TV series.

I offered to help him write story synopses, bios, fact sheets, and feature stories based on whatever comprised each week's episode. Before long that helping hand became a necessity, and with Michael's assistance I was upped to working as a full-fledged publicist and joining the Publicists Guild. I had fallen into a job and career that was made for me and I was ready to learn from the best.

One particular Disney publicist on staff who exemplified a "Hollywood press agent" to me was Arlene Ludwig. She had joined the company in its New York office in 1962, moved to Burbank several years later, and remained with the company for over five decades, retiring in 2013.

Arlene is a true professional, and one with a very special Disney birthright. Her father, Irving Ludwig, was also with Disney, joining the organization in 1940 as a film distribution executive. Working directly with Walt Disney (and beyond), he was responsible for launching such Disney films as *Fantasia*, *Mary Poppins*, and *101 Dalmatians*. He was also instrumental in creating Disney's film delivery company, Buena Vista Distribution, and served as its president from 1959 until 1980, when he retired as one of Hollywood's most respected business executives. Between Arlene and her father, the two Ludwig family members clocked nearly a century with The Walt Disney Company.

Arlene had a way with celebrities and was tasked with setting them up for interviews with TV, radio, and print outlets to support whatever film was being promoted. When the unit publicist assigned to a particular project completed their PR tasks (often working on film locations and on set), the actors were handed over to Arlene who then created a media agenda to promote that particular project. She also traveled on publicity tours and served as the point person managing the Hollywood Foreign Press. I remember many young actors destined to become big stars, like Rick Schroder and Jodie Foster, running in and out of Arlene's office as kids.

But in the late 70s and early 80s, Walt Disney Productions was not considered a major player in the movie-making arena. Of course, it was still highly regarded as the king of the animated film genre, although its output during that era was not the most memorable with such titles as *The Rescuers*, *The Fox and the Hound*, and *The Black Cauldron*. The company did score a home run, however, when it decided to commemorate a very important occasion, Mickey's 50th Anniversary. Arlene was on the scene in 1978 to kick off the celebration with Mickey's Whistle-Stop Tour.

She recalled, "We had a big Hollywood send-off party, with myriad press in attendance, at Union Station in Los Angeles. At the end of the evening's festivities Mickey got onboard a special Amtrak train that would take him on a whistle-stop tour across the country. I was fortunate to be part of the Disney group accompanying Mickey on tour. This was at a time when Mickey Mouse was rarely ever seen outside of a Disney theme park. For people to see him in person as he passed through little towns all the way from the west to the east coast was thrilling for them, especially the kids."

As they chugged through cities and towns along the way, Mickey stood on the open rear section of the caboose waving to the crowds that came out at all times of the day and night to see him pass by.

Another more successful side of the company back in the late 1970s was the theme parks—Disneyland had opened in 1955 and Walt Disney World in 1971. The company was active in television as well, with its long-running Sunday night *Wonderful World of Disney* series. But overall, the Disney Studio was considered small-time when it came it producing hit live-action films for adults. It was stuck in the "kids only" category and couldn't figure out how to extend its brand beyond that demographic. In fact, the studio was so laid back in its pursuit to aggressively compete with the big players in Hollywood that it was often referred to as "the country club".

Ludwig remembered those slower-paced days when she worked closely with the "Disney" era roster of stars such as Helen Hayes, Pearl Bailey, Shelley Winters, Ernest Borgnine, Roddy McDowall, Phyllis Diller, Dean Jones, Tim Conway, Don Knotts, Cloris Leachman, and David Niven. Then Michael and Frank arrived at the company.

"I remember when Michael and Frank came in," she said. Eisner had been president and CEO of Paramount Pictures, and Frank Wells, vice chairman of Warner Bros. "They got all of us out of our offices to personally meet them in front of the studio theatre." The new team soon proceeded to do a lot of housecleaning of the old regime, but they were top moviemakers and they were going to run Disney like a Hollywood studio should be run. The result? "They brought new life to Disney and it was reborn," recalled Ludwig.

Shortly after taking on his new role at Disney, Eisner brought in a third top executive, Jeffrey Katzenberg, who had served as president of

Production under Eisner's leadership at Paramount. Katzenberg was hired as Disney Studio chairman to specifically focus on revitalizing the company's film division. Katzenberg quickly put a slate of new films on the studio's agenda, providing the Publicity folks with great new products to market.

Ludwig said, "I'd say we moved up in the world starting with the movie *Down and Out in Beverly Hills*. The new regime embraced outside-of-Disney writers and directors instead of using the same people who had worked on so many Disney films. That just stopped working for us. Michael, Frank, and Jeffrey rejuvenated our film business on every level."

Under Katzenberg's leadership, Film Marketing became nothing short of brilliant in how it strategically positioned, advertised, publicized, and launched major marketing campaigns.

Their astonishing output laid the groundwork that fed all the other Disney business units that would ultimately cross-promote with the movie product. Disney's enviable string of box office successes in the Eisner, Wells, and Katzenberg era ultimately brought in hundreds of millions, and in some cases billions, of dollars in corporate profits.

Ludwig said, "It was very exciting because suddenly we had names like Bette Midler, Nick Nolte, Richard Dreyfuss, Julia Roberts, and Robin Williams. Disney had never really had that level of stars on their roster."

Of course, there were some major stars that spanned the old Disney era vs. the new Eisner/Wells/Katzenberg era spectrum, such as Julie Andrews who has remained a Ludwig friend for over forty years: "I met Julie for the first time at JFK Airport in New York. It was the early sixties when I was still working out of the New York Disney office. Julie's trip to the East Coast was in conjunction with PR for *Mary Poppins*. She was the dearest, sweetest person, and so warm. We stayed in touch over the years and nearly forty years later when she starred in Disney's *The Princess Diaries*, we picked up our friendship."

But before any of that happened, I was learning how to be a publicist myself from Michael Russell, my new boss in the Publicity Department. He was very congenial, as any publicist should be, and a master marketer although sometimes the "marketing" called for him to take on unexpected tasks. He reminded me of one such incident that happened in the late seventies: "It was about 7 am on a Saturday morning and I was sleeping when I got a phone call from Tom Wilhite [the publicity director at the time]. He said I had forty minutes to get to the studio and pick up a model of the spaceship used in the soon-to-be-released film, *The Black Hole*, take it to the airport, get on a plane with it in hand, and carry it to New York.

The movie prop was needed there right away for a high-profile promotional presentation that was to take place.

Throwing on a pair of jeans, t-shirt, and sneakers, Mike quickly headed out the door, drove to the studio and picked up the model, then raced to Los Angeles International Airport where two first class seats to New York City were waiting. One was for Mike, and the other for the spaceship.

The film *Never Cry Wolf* was another project for Mike that presented some unusual circumstances. He was serving as the unit publicist on what was to be a very prestigious production for Disney in the early eighties. *Never Cry Wolf* starred Charles Martin Smith as a government biologist sent into the wilderness to study the caribou population.

As the unit publicist, it was Mike's job to be on-set to conduct interviews with the film's actors, director, producer, etc., as well as to direct PR photography needs and handle any local press interviews. He would also write the complete press kit for the film. But the shoot location was not exactly the most desirable: to be on scene, Mike had to travel to Nome, Alaska, and the Yukon in the dead of winter.

Being a native Californian, Mike was more accustomed to playing tennis in the sunshine than snowmobiling in the frozen north. He had absolutely no warm clothes needed to make the trip. But being at the Disney Studio, there was an easy fix.

"We called the Wardrobe Department to find out if they had anything I could use," he explained. Mike was about the size of actor Dean Jones, who was noted for starring in the *Herbie, the Love Bug* series of films about the famous Volkswagen Beetle with its own personality. "Wardrobe still had Jones' cold weather clothes that he wore in a Disney film called *Snowball Express* that takes place at a ski resort in the Rocky Mountains." Mike was outfitted with winter parkas, woolen scarves, gloves, sweaters, and even boots. He stayed really warm.

I can't thank Michael Russell enough for giving me the opportunity to become a publicist. That one move led to all the wonderful work I ultimately got to do at Disney. He was, in fact, the mentor who launched my twenty-plus-year adventure inside the Disney marketing machine.

CHAPTER TWO

Marketing is Everything and Everything is Marketing

My days in Publicity at The Walt Disney Studios were the best thing that could have ever happened to a girl with stars in her eyes from Brooklyn. I so enjoyed my job, especially interviewing the actors and actresses starring in the Disney TV shows that I covered, whether it was in conjunction with a movie of the week or a new pilot for a series.

Friends would sometimes ask me if I got nervous about conducting the Q&As. My answer was clearly no, never. I was in total control. In truth, those sessions made me feel a little bit like Barbara Walters.

I often conducted my interviews over lunch in the Coral Room, an executive dining room adjacent to the Disney commissary that was very upscale with linen-covered tables along with waitress and menu service. My favorite item on the menu was the Rosie Salad. Anyone who ever frequented that dining room no doubt remembers it well. Akin to a Caesar salad but with large, plump shrimp and a delicious "secret recipe" dressing, it was the most popular item on the menu.

I interviewed many celebrities of the day over a Rosie Salad in that room, among them Mickey Rooney, Shirley Jones, Margaret O'Brien, Dean Jones, Tim Conway, Don Knotts, Hayley Mills, Ron Howard, Delta Burke, Janis Paige, and so many more including a host of behind-the-scenes talent—directors, producers, and animated character voices.

My interviews translated into myriad feature stories that I wrote and were distributed nationally to TV editors, with photos, in the hope they would run the stories as is, request an interview with the person showcased, and/or run the photo on the cover of their weekly TV book that was inserted inside the Sunday edition of their publications. This was in addition to my pitching celebrity interviews with our featured show's stars to key press in LA and around the country. Those interviews were completed via phone (if outside of LA) or over lunch with the media person if local. My job was to guide the discussion so whatever show we were promoting got a fair share of the conversation, and of course, to pay the lunch tab.

I also traveled to TV shoots, covering the publicity for such events as the TV special celebrating the 10th anniversary of Walt Disney World that was shot on location in Orlando, Florida. I was there to interview the cast—Ricky Schroder, Eileen Brennan, and Michael Keaton—and work with the production photographer to make sure we got the images we needed to promote the show, and get on-the-set media coverage from local press.

What I learned, from a marketing perspective, was the Disney way to do things, which I believe is the right way to do things. Marketing, of course, as mentioned earlier, is comprised of publicity, advertising, and promotions, with a variety of sub-groups that support each of them. While publicity was my beat, my interaction with all spokes in the marketing wheel was shaping my understanding of how it all came together.

Another aspect of my job was to nurture relationships with the media who reported for print, TV, and radio outlets. After all, the object of the game was to get them to write the most positive pieces about whatever was being promoted at the time. We always got the press what they needed, whether it was the interview, the special photo, or whatever. To this day, I have friendships with a number of journalists I first met back then. An important rule of marketing learned: maintain positive relationships with the press. It goes a long way.

My workload also included attending and working Disney movie premieres, parties that celebrated a particular film, and numerous special events. I saw, up-close-and-personal, master Disney marketers at work during these times. I absorbed how they handled the media, celebrities, and high-profile company executives.

I also occasionally traveled on tour with a TV or film star to do live interviews all over the country. For example, I spent three weeks on tour with actress Pam Grier, best known for such non-Disney films as *Foxy Brown* and *Fort Apache, The Bronx*. In this case, she was one of the stars in Disney's live-action feature film adaptation of Ray Bradbury's book *Something Wicked This Way Comes*.

Pam and I traveled the country, from coast to coast, on an airplane every day, promoting the movie. Pam did TV, radio, and print interviews from early morning to early evening in each city on our well-planned agenda. Following the last interview of the day we were off to the airport and on to the next city to do it all over again the next day. While it may seem glamorous, it was in reality quite a grind, but if with the right person, a fun one. My job was to make sure we got everywhere on time and that Pam got everything she needed. Thankfully, we got along great and it was a pleasure to be able to spend that much time with her. It's not always that way.

I remember spending a week on the road with an actor named Pat Buttram, best remembered for playing the role of "Mr. Haney" in the mid-1960s sitcom, *Green Acres*. He was touring for Disney as one of the animated character voices in the film *The Fox and the Hound*. Nothing I could do made Mr. Buttram happy. It was the longest week I ever had.

In 1982 Disney released *Tron*, a science fiction film that takes place inside the digital world of a video game. It was quite ahead of its time for the early eighties and has since taken on a cult following. But back then, although lauded for its visually stunning computer-animated sequences, the film was met with lukewarm reviews for its story.

The Publicity Department went to great lengths to create a positive "buzz" about the film prior to its release. One of the ways they did so was to send out several publicists (including me) across the country carrying a 16mm reel of film that highlighted the most striking moments of the computer generated "game" sequences.

After flying to Dubuque, Iowa, I rented a car and made my way, from key city to key city, and then finally to New York, visiting film journalists along the way and screening the film sequences for them. It was a great marketing concept at the time. Today, of course, a digital file would be sent and the journalist could review it on his or her computer, iPad, or cell phone. Back then, it took a lot more work, but it also cemented media relationships in a face-to-face way.

Probably the most significant event of my Disney career was in 1980 when I was named the publicist for an NBC television special called *The Mouseketeer Reunion* celebrating the 25th anniversary of the landmark children's television series, the *Mickey Mouse Club*.

The show was videotaped at the Disney Studio and starred almost all the people who were original Mouseketeers as children. Over the three-year course of the series, there were thirty-nine Mouseketeers. However, most of us remember those who appeared on the show on a daily basis including Bobby Burgess, Cubby O'Brien, Karen Pendleton, Tommy Cole, Darlene Gillespie, Sharon Baird, Lonnie Burr, Doreen Tracey, and of course, Annette Funicello.

I was not the original publicist for the show; that role belonged to a colleague of mine, Missy Sutton. She had created a wonderful national PR campaign to "Find the Missing Mouseketeers" when Disney was putting the show together. Many of the "mice" had been out of contact with the studio for a very long time and thus the PR outreach was not only a sensational idea to generate pre-show publicity, but helped track down almost all the Mouseketeers. The story spread like wildfire and was aired on hundreds of local TV stations, highlighted in major newspapers, and even generated a major story in *People* magazine.

Missy was a great publicist and working very hard on the project when an actors' strike hit Hollywood and every TV show in town was shut down, including *The Mouseketeer Reunion*, for three months. Missy was pregnant and soon to deliver. A new publicist was needed to take over the reins. That's where I came in, and how lucky I was!

Because of my involvement with that particular NBC special with the Mouseketeers, in the years to come I would often (and continue to be) called upon to spearhead a group of Mouseketeers (Bobby, Sharon, Cubby, Karen, Doreen, Darlene, Cheryl, Tommy, and Sherry Alberoni, who had joined the show in its second season) to promote many Disney events such as Mickey's 60th and Disneyland's 35th anniversaries, among a host of others. The Mouseketeers also starred in live shows at Disneyland for many years and were often involved in parades and meet-and-greet events. We spent a great deal of time together, traveled together, and just had a lot of fun.

Who knew that wanting to be a Mouseketeer as a child would almost end up coming true for me some twenty-five years later and lead to 35-year friendships that I treasure to this day. Plus, in 1995, I had the privilege to write the definitive book on the Mouseketeers, *The Official Mickey Mouse Club Book*, released by Hyperion, Disney's publishing arm. Meeting and working with that group changed my life.

Splash, the first film released under Disney's "adult" banner, Touchstone Pictures, starred Tom Hanks and Daryl Hannah, and was the last publicity project I was involved in at the studio. I was moving on to Disneyland, thirty-five miles south in Anaheim, having accepted the position of supervisor of Publicity. My minimal involvement in *Splash*, however, was interesting.

Splash was a love story about a man and a mermaid. My task was to accompany Daryl Hannah to a special photo shoot that she had with George Hurrell, a very famous "glamour" photographer of Hollywood stars, particularly those of the 1930s and 40s. Joan Crawford, Clark Gable, Bette Davis, Errol Flynn, Humphrey Bogart, James Cagney, Carole Lombard, Jean Harlow, and Rita Hayworth are just a few of those photographed by Hurrell. Now it was Hannah's turn, and glamorous she became.

We arrived at the Hollywood photo session, with Daryl dressed casually in jeans and sneakers, no makeup, and with her hair pulled back in a ponytail. But soon a remarkable transition occurred. With hairstylist, makeup man, and wardrobe coordinator awaiting, Hannah was transported back in time as a glamorous and stunning 1940s era "movie star" who might have just stepped out of Cary Grant's arms. The photos were impeccably lit and composed and the results were stunning.

This particular marketing angle was to broaden the scope of publicity for the film by placing the photos in upscale glamour and fashion publications that indeed enabled the promotion for *Splash* to extend well beyond the traditional Disney family audience. Of course, it was just one marketing device among myriad others to reach an adult audience, and it worked very well. *Splash* was a big hit.

After six very happy and very informative years learning the ins and outs of film and TV publicity, I was off to Disneyland. I got there just as Michael Eisner and Frank Wells joined the company. Disney was soon to be launched into the marketing stratosphere.

CHAPTER THREE

The Happiest Place on Earth

As a kid, I never thought I would visit Disneyland, three thousand miles away from where I lived in Brooklyn, New York. But, in 1984 I was hired as supervisor of Publicity for the park. And the icing on the cake was that I had the best workplace location imaginable. My office was in the park, above the attraction Great Moments With Mr. Lincoln in the Main Street Opera House. My window looked out on Town Square, the area one first encounters when walking into Walt Disney's original Magic Kingdom. The view from my window was amazing. I could peer out and see guests mingling with Disney characters, watch the parades go by my window every day, and view a great deal of joy happening at any moment. I miss that office.

The year 1984 was seminal for Disney. That's when Michael Eisner and Frank Wells joined the organization after an attempted hostile takeover of what was then known as Walt Disney Productions. Prior to that time, in fact since the passing of Walt Disney in 1966, creativity in the company seemed stalled. Rather than push new ideas, managers were often heard asking, "What Would Walt Do?" Even Roy E. Disney, Walt's nephew and the last Disney family member to serve on-staff at the studio, was disenchanted.

Roy had begun his Disney career in the 1950s as an assistant director, writer, and cinematographer, starting with Disney's first (and only) True-Life Fantasy, *Perri*. He became a production coordinator and then a producer for a number of the Disney television shows. In 1967, he was elected to the company's board of directors. Roy remained at the studio until 1977 when he resigned (although he retained his board seat) because "I just felt that creatively the company was not going anywhere interesting. It was very stifling."

Things did not get any better for the Disney organization in the next few years. From 1980 to 1983, as a 2009 Harvard Business School White Paper explained, the financial performance of Walt Disney Productions deteriorated as well. It was incurring heavy costs at that time in order to finish EPCOT Center (Walt's original plan for an "experimental prototype community of tomorrow"), which opened at Walt Disney World in 1982. It was also investing in the development of a new cable venture, The Disney Channel, launched in 1983. Film division performance remained erratic.

As corporate earnings stagnated, Roy E. Disney decided to step away from the company his uncle and father had founded. In March 1984, he severed all ties with the company and resigned from its board of directors.

In the following months, Walt Disney Productions was in turmoil as corporate raiders Saul Steinberg and Irwin Jacobs each made tender offers for the company with the intention of selling off its separate assets. Roy, perhaps to save the family name from disaster, re-emerged and organized a consortium of "white knight" investors to fend off the takeover attempts.

The white knights were led by Roy and Texas oil tycoon Sid Bass who made a $365 million investment in the company, rescuing it. Roy was reinstated to the board, and all hostile takeover attempts ended.

During the course of these developments, Roy was instrumental in re-structuring the company. Ron Miller (husband of Walt Disney's daughter, Diane) left his Disney CEO position. Roy believed that the company needed new life and new leadership and lobbied hard to bring Michael Eisner and Frank Wells onboard. Offers were made and they both accepted, despite never having worked together before. The pair were named chairman and CEO, and president and COO, respectively. Roy returned as chairman of Walt Disney Feature Animation and was named vice-chairman of the board.

As Michael Eisner stated in his book *Working Together*, he and Wells hit it off right from the start: "From our first day in the office that fall, my partnership with Frank Wells taught me what it was like to work with somebody who not only protected the organization but protected me, advised me, supported me, and did it all completely selflessly. I'd like to think I did the same for Frank, as well as the company. We grew together, learned together, and discovered together how to turn what was in retrospect a small business into indeed a very big business."

In total, Eisner and Wells worked together at Disney for nearly ten years, but in 1984 they were just beginning. Moving from The Walt Disney Studios to Disneyland, it was a new beginning for me, too. And with Eisner and Wells' aggressive agenda for the company, I would soon find myself deeper inside the Disney marketing machine.

At the beginning of my tenure in Disneyland Publicity, the department did things in a limited way, at least to my way of thinking. I surely was an upstart when I arrived on the scene, wanting to push the PR envelope far beyond what was their usual routine by initiating strategies I had learned during my tenure at the studio. It was a struggle at first, but eventually the powers-that-be began to see the light and became more open-minded to new ideas, especially when they started to see results—more media ink, as they say.

The first big event that I got involved in at Disneyland was the celebration of Donald Duck's 50th anniversary, a joint venture between Disney corporate (as Donald represented the entire company) and the Disney theme parks where Donald Fauntleroy Duck resides. The actual 50th anniversary date was June 9, 1984, as Donald had been "born" on June 9, 1934, with his motion picture debut in the Silly Symphony cartoon *The Wise Little Hen*.

A very aggressive (and very fun) marketing campaign was created under the leadership of Jack Lindquist, a long-time Disney executive and genius marketer who was known for his big ideas. At that time he headed Marketing for Disneyland and Walt Disney World, and created the Donald Duck anniversary concept with Jim Garber, Vice-President of Marketing for the Disney Studio. I oversaw the publicity for the celebration.

Until this time, animated character focus had always been squarely on the big cheese himself, Mickey Mouse. However, a 50th anniversary was quite a milestone. The company decided it was time to turn some attention to Donald Duck, who not only had a rich film history, but a loyal following of his own, with an "irascible" personality that was perfect fodder for media attention. As Jack Lindquist said of the commemoration: "Donald is a character very much into oneupmanship so we wanted him to have one-up on Mickey Mouse, whose 50th Birthday Whistle Stop Tour was a national event."

Lindquist and Garber came up with the idea to send Donald on his own whistle-stop tour, but unlike Mickey's Amtrak journey, Donald was to travel on a multi-city tour on his own 727 jet, accompanied by a host of Disney characters and one very special guest, Clarence "Ducky" Nash, the original voice of Donald Duck.

A good part of the strength of the marketing plan was having Nash involved as the literal mouthpiece for the campaign. It was the one of the first times that a character voice was placed into the media spotlight, as Walt Disney had always felt it important for those folks to remain behind the scenes. But Nash had voiced Donald for almost 50 years, in over 120 shorts and films, and it was time for him to step out in a big way. Of course, Donald Duck went on to become one of the most famous cartoon characters in the world, and a great part of this was due to Nash's distinctive voice. It may well be one of the most recognizable character voices in film history.

To realize their concept, the team of Lindquist and Garber made a deal with PSA (Pacific Southwest Airlines) and acquired a jet aircraft to use for the tour. To prepare for the promotion, they had the plane repainted and affixed with a gigantic flying Donald Duck image along the entire fuselage with the words "Happy 50th Birthday Donald Duck".

On Wednesday, June 6, 1984, a contingent of Disney characters along with Ducky Nash; his wife, Margie; Jack Lindquist; Bill Justice, one of Disney's key animators of Donald Duck and Chip 'n Dale shorts; Paula Sigman, from the Disney Archives; and a group of behind-the-scenes cast members from Disneyland's Entertainment Division and Studio Promotions departed from Burbank Airport on the plane that was dubbed "Duck One".

With a grand media sendoff, the plane departed for a four-day whirlwind tour. To capture as much media attention as possible in each city, in as short a time as possible, the celebratory trip was uniquely designed. Rather than have Donald, Ducky Nash, and the rest of the troupe arrive in a city, check into a hotel, and follow a regular media agenda visiting newspapers, TV, and radio stations, the "Duck One" tour was only scheduled to make short stops at local airports.

Once there, "Happy Birthday Donald Duck" events took place right on the tarmac. Disney Studio Publicity had made all the arrangements in advance working with local contacts in each city to have school children invited to meet and celebrate Donald's birthday at the airport. Of course, TV, radio, and print media were invited as well.

The tour included 13 airport celebrations in San Jose, Sacramento, Eugene, Seattle, Salt Lake City, Denver, St. Louis, New York, Boston, Chicago, Orlando, Atlanta, and Dallas, before returning home to Orange County, California. As part of the fun, as "Duck One" made its approach to the airports, an audio track was played to the waiting crowd that featured Disney characters Chip 'n' Dale as pilot and co-pilot going through a comedic routine to land the plane.

Once down and in position, Donald Duck, Nash, and a host of Disney characters would step up to a platform stage set with balloons, birthday decorations, and microphone, and welcome the kids there to see them. Then a big birthday cake would be moved in and everyone would sing "Happy Birthday" to Donald, giving media free rein to take photos. Usually within 30 minutes or so, everyone was loaded back onboard for the hop to the next city where everyone would to do it all again. Media that wanted a more up-close-and-personal interview with Nash were provided specially designed "Duck One" boarding passes and invited to fly to the next city with the troupe.

Nash, who was a lively 79 years old when this event took place, was a delightful man who loved "doing" Donald's voice and did so at every opportunity, especially when children were around. This lovely gentleman might be having a normal chat with someone and suddenly Donald Duck would pop out of his mouth. It never failed to bring smiles to faces young and old alike. I particularly remember being in New York during the 50th anniversary tour with Clarence and his wife. She was the only person who didn't call him Ducky: "I call him 'honey' because I knew him before he was a duck," she explained.

We were in a packed elevator and all was quiet. Suddenly, Donald Duck made a remark about how crowded the elevator was. Heads turned and stared at Ducky like he was nuts. Stopping at the next floor, "Donald" said his "excuse me's" making his way out. I was trailing behind as someone remarked, "He must like Donald Duck." I replied, "He *is* Donald Duck."

New York City was one of the special stops on the tour route. We were there for two days and had a gigantic birthday celebration in Rockefeller Plaza. Local dignitaries, celebrities, and marching bands welcomed the irascible Disney character. As part of the festivities, Donald was presented with an honorary membership card from the Screen Actors Guild that was also celebrating its 50th anniversary in 1984. That presentation was tied into the Donald Duck Film Festival that opened immediately following the Rockefeller Plaza event at the Guild Theater on 50th street.

Saturday, June 9, 1984, Donald's actual birthday, offered yet another opportunistic media event as the duck, Nash, and the Disney character crew triumphantly returned from their "whistle stop" airplane tour, landing at El Toro Marine Base in California. Upon arrival, Donald reviewed the troops before been driven, by police-escorted motorcade, back home to Disneyland where he was welcomed by a ticker-tape parade.

More publicity events were also on the roster both before and after the big Duck One tour. In May of that year, during the annual Armed Forces Day Parade in Torrance, California, Donald received his honorable discharge. Donald had joined the military in the 1941 cartoon short, *Donald Gets Drafted*, although he had never been discharged. Attired in a WWII Army uniform (thanks to Disneyland Costuming), the feisty fowl was officially discharged with honors as Sgt. Duck by the parade's grand marshal, Lt. General Arthur E. Brown, Jr., United States Army.

Also in May, one of our biggest Donald's 50th PR creations was having Donald place his webbed duck prints in the forecourt of world-famous Mann's Chinese Theater alongside such Hollywood legends as John Wayne, Clark Gable, and Marilyn Monroe. A massive crowd of media covered the ceremony, with photos being circulated worldwide. Another event that month had Los Angeles Mayor Tom Bradley proclaiming Donald Duck Day in the City of Angels and presenting him with a special proclamation.

All in all, Donald Duck's 50th Birthday Celebration was one of the biggest corporate marketing events that the studio had ever undertaken up until that time. In addition to those discussed, other marketing highlights included:

- The daily Donald Duck 50th Birthday Parade at both Disneyland and Walt Disney World, new Donald's 50th merchandise items incorporated into sales venues, and Donald Duck surprise giveaways.
- Donald Duck Orange Juice tie-in campaign.
- *Donald Duck's 50th Birthday* prime-time national network TV special on CBS, hosted by Dick Van Dyke.
- National tie-in promotion with Smuckers/Skippy/Best Foods.
- *Donald Duck: 50 Years of Happy Frustration* book.
- *Donald and His Nephews* book, from Abbeville Press.
- Coca-Cola national promotion.
- One-hundred-and-thirty Disney licensees produced Donald Duck products. Most featured the Happy Birthday Donald logo.
- Western Publishing produced a Donald Duck book promotion and added twelve new books, puzzles, and games to the Donald product line.
- Grolier produced Donald Duck books, commemorative plates, and figurines.
- Rainbow created limited edition Donald Duck lithographs.
- Disney's original limited-edition portfolio of Donald Duck cels and collector's aluminum Donald were sold.
- Happy Birthday Donald Duck Sweepstakes was generated for the retail trade.
- Donald Duck and Mousercise meet-and-greets took place at malls.
- Donald Duck appeared on *Good Morning America*.
- Donald Duck film festivals and retrospectives were held across the country.
- *Mickey's Christmas Carol*, featuring Donald Duck, began annual network television broadcasts.
- Retail stores held a Donald Duck Sweepstakes featuring 25 grand prize trips to EPCOT.
- New York's Thanksgiving Day Parade, Philadelphia's Thanksgiving Day Parade, and Hollywood's Thanksgiving Day Parade saluted Donald Duck.
- Donald Duck appeared on the City of Glendale float in the Rose Parade.

Donald Fauntleroy Duck was having a good year, but there was more to come.

CHAPTER FOUR

Donald and His Flock

Walt Disney World really had something special up their sleeve to celebrate the duck's five-decade history. It was a crazy idea hatched by long-time Walt Disney World publicity guru, Charlie Ridgway

"We were sitting around thinking what we could do for Donald Duck's 50th birthday," said Ridgway. "We said, okay, we'll have a parade and we'll do some decorations for it. And I said, 'What if we could train 50 white ducks to follow Donald Duck down the street in the parade?' And everybody laughed and thought that was the silliest thing they ever heard. I thought we could get a great photo out of it."

While others may have scoffed, Ridgway pursued the idea. "I called the guy who was the head of Walt Disney World's Discovery Island at the time in charge of birds and things. He said he didn't know if we could do it, but he called some friends he knew in the bird business and they said that the training could be done, but the ducks would have to bond with Donald Duck from the time they're born."

That's all Ridgway needed to hear. He put the wheels in motion. "We arranged to have Donald go to Miami to a hatchery where a bunch of ducks were hatching out and we got some great footage of Donald down on the floor with them as they're coming out of the shell." Never one to let a marketing opportunity go by, Ridgway added, "That was covered by the Florida television stations.

Then we brought the ducklings back to Walt Disney World and put them out at the farm at Fort Wilderness because there was a petting area out there. While they were growing up every few days we would send Donald out there to play with them and throw out some lettuce and get them to follow him around. As they grew up and changed from little yellow ducklings to grown up white ducks they got closer and closer to Donald, eventually trailing him everywhere."

Moving forward, it was decided to put the ducks in Donald's 50th parade. "We built a small enclosure behind City Hall in Town Square that was by my office so we could keep an eye on the ducks," explained Ridgway. "I probably came up with the idea that as long as they were going to a party, they ought to have party hats on." The Walt Disney World Wardrobe Department figured out how to make birthday hats for them, but the problem became how do you get the hats to stay on their heads?

"The wardrobe guy came up with the idea of using Velcro," said Ridgway. "So they glued the Velcro onto the feathers on the top of the duck's heads and then you could stick the hat up there with a little rubber band on them that went under their chins."

Concerned that the ducks couldn't walk the whole long parade route, Marketing decided to develop a little float on which they could ride. Ridgway recalled that "We put a picket fence around the float so the ducks wouldn't fall off and a song was played that went quack, quack, quack. During the hotter weather when the ducks get warm they panted, so it looked like they were singing the quack, quack, quack. Then we said, okay, we have to have a birthday cake for them. They really liked corn, so we froze corn in the shape of a cake. We put the ducks on the lawn in front of the castle and they were very good about attacking it. The ducks were the hit of the parade all the time we celebrated Donald's 50th birthday. The reaction of the guests was wonderful."

But what happened to the ducks at the close of the Donald's 50th parade and celebration? "We decided we couldn't very well have the ducks for Thanksgiving dinner or anything like that when we got through with the event. We decided to give them away to major zoos around the country. At that point, we put velvet ribbons around their necks with nametags on them, taking the names of Disney characters. There was Snow White duck and Alice in Wonderland duck and so forth. The ducks were presented to different zoos wearing their hats and nametags."

The ducks all lived a very long and good life. They were popular in the zoos as having been the ducks in Donald's 50th birthday parade at Walt Disney World. Of course, giving the ducks away to zoos opened the door to even more publicity, as Ridgway soon found out, "Every time we gave a duck away to a zoo, and we did so all over the country, we got local TV, radio, and print publicity on it."

Ridgway was also involved in a new concept that turned out to be a marketing bonanza when it came to publicity at Walt Disney World. He explained that "This idea came about pre-Eisner and Wells in conjunction with the opening of EPCOT Center in October 1982, and the thousands of global press that we invited to cover it. Jack Lindquist came up with the idea of maybe setting up a direct television connection between the major media coming down to the park. We looked into a cable possibility, but discovered that was going to be pretty expensive. Then we said, 'Well, what about satellite?' And the powers-that-be said, 'What's satellite?' But in look-ing into the possibility of broadcasting live via a satellite connection, they learned that, yes, they could have a satellite uplink. With Jack's backing as the head of Marketing for Walt Disney Attractions, we decided to do it.

While they were setting it up they checked with local stations around the country to find out if they would be interested in doing live uplinks from the grand opening of EPCOT Center. Having long-time relationships with the stations, the marketing folks called some of their friends who were news directors. They all reacted to the notion in a positive way. Ridgway said that "It was quite a novel way to do things back then to have local television guys go out and do live remotes from so far away. It was a major breakthrough and we kind of discovered it by accident."

According to Ridgway, thirty-six stations accepted the invitation to go down to Walt Disney World Resort and do live remotes: "We flew them in and sometimes they brought their own crew and sometimes we provided the crew. We had set up major communication facilities with on-site edit bays so they could go in and cut their stories."

The facilities were set up on EPCOTs opening night. Each of the stations put together a five-minute segment for their 6 pm news. Since Orlando is on the East Coast, the Disney World Resort broadcast team was dealing with three time zones that had to be ready to accommodate 12 stations per hour so that they could cover the 36 stations on-hand in three hours. Ridgway said: "One of the things that happened right after the stations broadcasted their segments was that the switchboards at the stations lit up like Christmas trees with people calling in wanting to know more about EPCOT. In several cases, they had their reporters stay down for the entire week and do a segment every night. We had the satellite in place and they could do it."

And they did.

CHAPTER FIVE

Eisner and Wells Invade the Magic Kingdoms

On Monday morning, September 24, 1984, Michael Eisner and Frank Wells officially walked onto the lot of The Walt Disney Studios as CEO and president, respectively, for the first time taking over the reins of what was then Walt Disney Productions (the name was changed to The Walt Disney Company in 1986).

Former Paramount film executive Jeffrey Katzenberg soon came aboard as chairman of Walt Disney Studios. His focus was to develop a new slate of Disney live-action films and revive the company's Feature Animation division. That task was guided under the leadership of Roy E. Disney, who had accepted the position of chairman of Walt Disney Feature Animation.

Just days after their arrival at Disney, Eisner and Wells were exploring Disneyland, visiting the shops and riding the attractions, while peppering the park executives who accompanied them with myriad questions about everything. They were insatiably inquisitive.

After reviewing the ins and outs of Disneyland, they stopped by every departmental office to introduce themselves to the executives and support staff in Marketing, Entertainment, Operations, Merchandise, Foods, Security, etc. Then they flew to Walt Disney World and repeated the scenario, albeit on a much larger scale based on the size and scope of the Orlando property.

After just a few months on the job, one of the first changes to come about was the expansion of Disneyland's hours of operation. Although now it seems ridiculous to think that the park could be closed two days a week, from 1958 to 1985 Disneyland was closed on Mondays and Tuesdays in the off-season. The busy seasons were considered summer (Memorial Day through Labor Day), Christmas (a two-week period beginning the week before Christmas and ending New Year's Day), and Spring Break. Off-season was everything else. Nineteen-eighty-five marked the first time Disneyland would follow a 365-day operational calendar.

Disneyland Advertising was also one of the first aspects of marketing that was greatly influenced by Eisner and Wells, and they wasted no time getting into it right from the start. Ron Kollen, then the advertising manager for the park, said: "The big difference before and after Michael and Frank was that before our advertising was small-time and very local up until 1984. Our budgets were small and the focus had been on promoting the park through publicity and promotions rather than advertising because advertising cost money that the powers-that-be were reluctant to spend. But the day that Michael and Frank took over, that drastically changed."

Anne White, who worked closely with Kollen and oversaw Creative Services for the park, agreed with him. "It was very exciting when Michael and Frank came on board. I was in charge of all marketing graphics for the park and supported the needs of advertising, publicity, promotions, and many other marketing extensions of those areas. We would design pins, buttons, special tickets, logos, anything that required special graphics. When Michael and Frank arrived on the scene, we were coming off a slow period. Everything we did up to that point was focused on the local area rather than expanding our capacity to reach consumers nationally through our advertising."

Although the period pre-Eisner and Wells had been less than aggressive for White's department, it was no less creative from a Disney point-of-view.

She recalled a presentation in the late 1970s when she and a marketing cohort, Betty Birney (now a bestselling author of children's books), decided to bring a bit of fun to their pitch. "We had created the advertising art and copy for the opening of Big Thunder Mountain Railroad in Frontierland. We were preparing to present it to the head of Walt Disney Attractions, Dick Nunis; Jack Lindquist, who headed marketing; and several other high-profile executives, including the Disney company CEO at that time, Card Walker.

"I don't know what possessed us" she said, "but Betty and I decided to make our presentation in theme. We went out and bought kid's cowboy hats and holsters with pistols and wore them to showcase our artwork and ad copy for what was to be a new Western-themed thrill ride. We were so enthusiastic and wearing our little hats with the strings pulled up under our chins and sporting our guns and holsters. Where else but at Disneyland could you do this and not get fired? They loved the presentation and our ad campaign was approved."

While ideas like "dressing up" to make a presentation were not exactly the everyday norm, injecting that sense of fun into a meeting was welcomed at Disneyland, White explained: "You had no fear about doing things like that because the culture and the environment in which we worked made it okay."

Working at Disneyland also had other perks for White that inspired creativity when needed. "Sometimes I'd take my staff out into the park and we'd hop on the train at the Main Street Station and take over the caboose to brainstorm ideas for whatever we working on. Just being in that atmosphere brought out the best in us."

On the other hand, when White was having a bad day she sometimes headed out to the park by herself, got on Space Mountain (a wild roller coaster ride through outer space), and screamed at the top of her lungs while speeding around curves and plunging through drops: "And then I'd just pull myself up, put my shoulders back, and head back to my office re-invigorated."

According to White, Eisner and Wells embraced that culture: "I remember when they came to Disneyland for a walk-through just days after they arrived at the company. They visited all the different departments in the park and personally introduced themselves to everyone. It was obvious that they wanted to put their whole heart and souls into the job."

For both Kollen and White, new advertising directives raised everyone's game to new heights. Ron Kollen said, "They challenged us all to do better and be smarter. One of the first things we did was hire Young & Rubicam, a very high-profile ad agency, to work with us. For the first time we began doing national advertising and more types of things that Walt Disney World was already doing. Almost overnight, they elevated our mission."

Raising Disneyland's advertising to a higher level was not just based on edicts from the top. Eisner and Wells got personally involved. Kollen explained, "I had to show Michael print ads every week. He also looked at all our TV commercials before they aired."

Wells jumped in a big way as well. "Before 1984, the parks were very Operations driven and it was often difficult for Marketing to do anything in-park without the Operations people signing off on it. That group, rightly so, was not marketing oriented, but Michael and Frank were. They understood that the two needed to be more closely aligned."

To form a greater alignment with all the park departments, Wells instructed Disneyland and Walt Disney World to put together a cross-divisional team, bringing together executives from each Park area: Operations, Advertising, Publicity, Promotions, Entertainment, Finance, etc. Wells said. "I want everyone in a room together. Let's look at what we're doing well and what we can do better. I also want to know what's the big idea. I really want to hear big ideas."

Thus, Disneyland created their group and named them the MAESTROS (Marketing And Entertainment Strategic Organization). Walt Disney World's assembly was called the MATADORS (Marketing Admissions Team Assigned to Disney Opportunity of Rapidly Succeeding).

Regular meetings were set and information and ideas were shared on how each idea might impact a particular department. Compromises were hashed out eye-to-eye across a conference table until issues were settled. It cemented relationships and brought a new clarity to everything going on behind the scenes. In fact, MAESTROS and MATADORS were indeed the forerunners for what became a much broader synergy operation that ultimately permeated the entire Disney Company.

Mike Davis, who headed the Entertainment division at the time, said: "After Disneyland's MAESTROS began meeting, the relationship among Marketing, Operations, and Entertainment became closer. Jack Lindquist decided to move Bob McTyre, who was brought in as an entertainment executive in the early eighties, to head what then became a joint Marketing/ Entertainment division. Then I became director of Entertainment, and a long-time Disneyland exec, Mark Feary, was named director of Marketing, both of us reporting to McTyre."

According to Davis, combining the two divisions multiplied and strengthened the resulting product for the Disneyland guest and brought greater marketing opportunities to the forefront. "There was a tremendous cohesiveness of creative talk when we were combined. In the theme park business, Marketing's job is to get people to the park. That's the number one simple truth. Entertainment's job was when they got there they had a great experience and they're excited enough to tell their friends and to come back. If you hit on both those points, you win."

Davis had a very good relationship with Eisner and Wells. He recalled this amusing story. "I remember one time when we were doing an event called the Disney Symphonic Spectacular that toured the country doing forty cities in eight weeks. In L.A. the venue was the Hollywood Bowl and Frank Wells was the onstage host. Handling all he had to do onstage, Frank's most important question to me was whether I wanted him to wear a tuxedo or a suit and tie. I told him a suit and tie would be the most appropriate attire. Wells then said, "You always put a kick line, like the Rockettes, into a lot of these shows. Is there going to be a kick line, because if there is I'd like to be part of it."' "Really?" "Yes, really," said Wells.

A kick line closed the show with the addition of one new dancer— Frank Wells.

It was not the only time the seemingly buttoned up Wells got into the fun of the Disney experience. One such story happened at Eisner and Wells' annual appearance at what was called the Disney Employee Forum. It was a meeting that was held on a soundstage at The Walt Disney Studios or other appropriate venue that could hold hundreds of Disney employees local to the Burbank headquarters of the company including nearby (Glendale) WED Enterprises (renamed Walt Disney Imagineering in 1986).

The gathering was also provided, via satellite feed, to Disneyland and Walt Disney World on closed circuit TV. It was always hosted by Eisner and Wells and a big deal from an internal company standpoint. It was anything but dry and boring. There were always surprises and unexpected goings-on.

Jeff Hoffman, a Burbank-based employee who then served as an executive at the Disney University (which handled cast activities, among other responsibilities), helped produce the annual Disney Employee Forum. He said, "The event was basically an internal update on "this is what's going on in the company, business unit by business unit, what's new and what's coming up from new movies to new park attractions". It was all about informing the employees and getting them excited about the company, to get their juices going and as a result create better cross-marketing promotions."

Some of the special surprises that happened through the years included bringing in the nuns from the movie *Sister Act* on the year of its release and having them perform the song "My God"; having the president of Disney Consumer Products, Bo Boyd, ride around the stage on a Disney branded tricycle; and showing a video of Michael Eisner calling Frank Wells out of a meeting to surprise him with a pie in the face (Eisner also got a pie in the face, from Goofy, when videotaping a TV intro for *The Wonderful World of Disney*).

Senior Disneyland Broadcast producer Tony Perri and his cameraman happened to be at the right place at the right time to shoot the footage of Wells getting hit with the pie. Perri recalled, "I was at the studio having just done a video interview with Eisner. My cameraman and I were packing our equipment and Eisner says to me, "Let's go see Frank, and bring the camera.""

Perri and his cameraman, not knowing what was to happen, did as they were told. Somewhere on the way to a conference room where Wells was attending a meeting, someone handed Eisner a pie. Arriving at the meeting room door with Eisner, Perri recalled that the cameraman was instructed to turn on the camera and start shooting. "Michael knocks on the door, Frank opens it, and pow!, Eisner hits him in the face with the pie. Frank always struck me as a serious guy and as soon as he got hit with the pie I sensed he wasn't happy, but after scooping the whipped cream out of his eyes, he seemed fine. Michael was hysterical."

The Disney Employee Forum also provided the backdrop for another uncharacteristic endeavor in which Wells was involved. He flew onstage with Tinker Bell. Yes, that's right, flew on stage. Jeff Hoffman said, "That happened the year we brought Tinker Bell back to Disneyland to kick off the fireworks as she had in the past. We thought what better way to market the return of Tinker Bell to the employees than to have Tinker Bell fly Frank onto the stage to open the event."

Wells, wearing a suit and tie, was fully willing to participate. He was put into a flying harness and Tinker Bell was readied in full costume. Hoffman continued, "We flew both of them from the back of soundstage 2 (where the forum was being held that year), right to the onstage podium."

As was Disney's way, an extra plus was added when Hoffman and crew had mirror balls installed and provided employees up in the rafters of the soundstage with bags of glitter to heighten the experience as Tink and Frank flew in. Needless to say, the audience loved it.

So much of what was presented at the annual Disney Employee Forum was meant to be entertaining and fun. Another example is when Richard Nanula, Disney Chief Finance Officer, would make his presentation. A finance presentation? Boring, one might think. But no, recalled Hoffman, it was done with Disney showmanship,.

One of the ways Richard made his point about the financial success of the company was to show a film of a little old couple. He would explain, through very funny visuals, how they had bought Disney stock on the day Disneyland opened in 1955 and how their small investment increased dramatically through the years via company success, stock splits, and ever-increasing value. By the end, they were millionaires living the high life. It was entertaining and clearly made its point.

All of what took place at the Disney Employee Forums was informational, but also very enjoyable at the same time. Hoffman said, "It was all about reinforcing that Disney is different. Entertainment, happiness, and creating magical experiences are what we infused in everything we did, even when addressing our own employees and cast members at the parks and resorts. That's who we were."

CHAPTER SIX

Marketing an Unlikely Anniversary

One of Disneyland's biggest celebrations came with the unlikely commemoration of its 30th anniversary in 1985. While not exactly a celebratory number, in the Disney marketing game no one was going to let such a minor detail stop them from touting it as the greatest, most stupendous celebration of all time.

One of my PR tasks for that event was to work with the park's Creative Services group to develop an imaginative Disneyland's 30th identity. They created a 30th anniversary logo that ultimately became the icon affixed to all marketing materials that year. Using the logo, newly designed Disneyland 30th stationery was created, a variety of products sporting the 30th design was developed, and even new cast member nametags sported the 30th logo.

Of course, an extravagant 30th year press kit was required for publicity use as well. I came up with the idea to have the overall kit be comprised of two press kits in one—the first kit with stories focusing on Disneyland's past, and the second on its present. The "past" and "present" materials were each enclosed in their own representative folders within the larger overall 30th folder designed in silver with the logo on the cover.

The "past" contained historical Disneyland material, including a key story about Disneyland's disastrous opening day on July 17, 1955, titled "Day One":

> The cars stretched bumper-to-bumper for seven miles on the Santa Ana Freeway in what police at the time called, "the worse traffic jam ever seen". The date was July 17, 1955, and the contingent of first-day invitees were on their way to Anaheim where Walt Disney, known for his creative genius in the motion picture industry, was about to unveil a new entertainment experience, his personal dream, Disneyland.
>
> Tickets for the invitational opening day event had been given to studio workers and those who had constructed the park, to press,

dignitaries, and celebrities. But as the gates opened a year after groundbreaking on the 160-acre orange grove, all was not quite ready.

Nearly 30,000 invited guests along with countless ticket counterfeiters poured through the gates to find long lines everywhere. Rides broke down shortly after opening and restaurants and refreshment stands ran out of food and drink. Fantasyland had to be temporarily closed due to a gas leak, workmen were still planting trees, and in some areas paint was wet to the touch. The blistering heat of the July day added to the distress as the spiked heels on women's shoes sank into the asphalt on Main Street, U.S.A.

Yet, Walt Disney was unaware of the chaotic situation. He was being shuttled from one part of the park to another for a live 90-minute television broadcast, *Dateline Disneyland*, showcasing his newly unveiled creation. Joined by co-hosts Bob Cummings, Art Linkletter, and a man destined to become president of the United States, Ronald Reagan, 90 million viewers witnessed the fantastic result of one man's dream come true. Celebrities on hand included Buddy Ebsen and Fess Parker, who entertained in Frontierland, along with Charlton Heston, Eve Arden, Maureen O'Hara, Frank Sinatra, Sammy Davis Jr., Kirk Douglas, Danny Thomas, Eddie Fisher, and Debbie Reynolds, among others. Also on hand were the Mouseketeers, an unknown group of youngsters yet three months away from making their television debut on a series that was to become a national children's viewing habit, the *Mickey Mouse Club*.

It wasn't until the following day, via press accounts, that Walt Disney became aware of the negative reaction to Disneyland. "Walt's Dream a Nightmare", "Park Can't Handle Opening Day Crush", "Disneyland Opens Amid Traffic Jams, Confusion", etc., declared headlines across the nation. Ever afterward, Walt Disney would refer to that fateful day as Black Sunday.

But as Hollywood columnist Sheila Graham reported after her first-day disappointments, "Don't be discouraged boys and girls, Walt Disney has always been a smart trader and I'm sure there will be some changes made."

And changes there were. Walt immediately summoned his staff and together they dealt with the problems of ride capacity, handling the flow of people through the park, relieving traffic jams and serving food more expeditiously. Walt spent his days and nights at Disneyland, observing guests, ride operators, waitresses, store clerks, and janitors, asking questions in a constant search to improve all aspects of what was emerging as the most successful venture of his accomplished career.

After only seven weeks of operation, Disneyland welcomed its one-millionth guest and at the end of its first fiscal year, 3.8 million visitors had been hosted. Black Sunday today seems but a distant memory to the success and popularity of the magical land that Walt Disney built. As he said in his dedication speech on that first day:

"To all who come to this happy place; welcome. Disneyland is your land. Here age relives fond memories of the past and here youth may savor the challenge and promise of the future. Disneyland is dedicated to the ideals, the dreams, and the hard facts that have created America with the hope that it will be a source of joy and inspiration to all the world."

Walt Disney's words are as true today as they were then and will be for future generations to come.

For the 30th, of course there had to be a great PR angle that would give Disneyland Publicity the opportunity to promote the celebration every day of that year, 1985. The big idea that served as the marketing anchor for the yearlong "birthday party" came from Disney's marketing master, Jack Lindquist. At the time he headed marketing for both Disneyland and Walt Disney World, and ultimately became Disneyland's first president. He retired from the company in 1993, but his out-of-the-box marketing concepts were always home runs.

In all my years at Disney I cannot think of one person who ever said an unkind word about Jack Lindquist. He is down to earth, was ever approachable, and would listen to anyone when it came to marketing ideas, from street sweepers in the park to executive colleagues. He always had a mischievous twinkle in his eye and you never knew what to expect. Long-time Walt Disney World marketing executive Phil Lengyel recalled, "Jack Lindquist is my idol. I remember before Eisner and Wells came onboard when we were getting ready to open EPCOT Center and we needed to pitch Card Walker, then the company CEO, on some extra programming money that we needed to do some newspaper advertising."

Lengyel flew to L.A. to participate in that meeting with Lindquist and Tom Elrod, his marketing boss, and to take Walker through their thinking. "I get to the studio and we had this meeting all set up for 9 am in Card's office where he was waiting to start the session. I get there and there's no Jack and there's no Tom. There I am and I've got my slide projector to click Card through this thing. Now I had only met him a couple of times so when I get to his office I reintroduce myself and make small talk for a few minutes. Still no Jack and Tom. Card finally says, "So what's going on?" and I decided I'd better start. So I take him through the stuff, just the two of us. And then he says, "Are you asking for money?" And I said, "Well, there's an element of budget to this..." And he said, "You're asking for money." I said, "Yes, I am." He got up, unplugged my slide projector, and walked out."

Lengyel rushed over to Lindquist's office and there he was sitting at his desk smiling from ear to ear. Lengyel said, "Where were you?" and Lindquist replied, "He threw you out, didn't he?" Lengyel said, "Yeah, where were you? You were supposed to protect me and help me." "Oh, I knew that was going to happen," Lindquist said. "I didn't need to see that." Lengyel said, "So what are we going to do?" "Oh, we're going to do it anyway." That was Jack Lindquist.

For Disneyland's 30th anniversary, Lindquist came up with a concept focusing on something called the "Gift Giver Extraordinaire". His proposal seemed so off-the-wall that he put his job on the line to get a buy-off to proceed with the idea. So what exactly was a Gift Giver Extraordinaire? Lindquist explains, "In late 1984 we had gone through the L.A. Olympics at Disneyland which turned out to be a bomb in terms of attendance and we were way under attendance projections at 9.2 million visitors. I knew in 1985 we had to do something spectacular. We didn't have a new attraction, and I started thinking about an anniversary. It was Disneyland's 30th year, but everyone told me that nobody celebrates a 30th anniversary. So what? Then I thought about cars because they're pretty universal and have both great male and female appeal. What if we gave away cars?"

But this wasn't the first time Lindquist had come up with an idea to use cars to entice people to a specific location. Before he started working at Disneyland (as the park's first advertising manager, two months after it opened in 1955), Lindquist worked for an L.A. ad agency and represented Kelvinator, a company that made washers, dryers, refrigerators, and other appliances.

He recalled, "Every week I had to come up with another gimmick to get customers to go down to a local appliance store that sold Kelvinator products and hopefully the salespeople could hook them in to buying a new item. I was always coming up with crazy stuff to make that work and one week I decided we would give away cars to people who would come down to the store to get an appraised value on the appliances they owned. I went out and bought twenty used cars at wholesale for $50 each. We did a local TV commercial that said, "Mom, how would you like a second car so you can take your kids to the doctor or go shopping?" In those days, nobody had a second car. Of course the kind of cars I bought were not exactly the cream of the crop. If they had one good side that would work because that's all we wanted to show to the camera."

Despite a few dents here and there on the cache of cars, Lindquist said that "the promotion worked so well I had to go out and buy 200 more!"

And so a Kelvinator promotion was the genesis of Lindquist's idea to give away cars (new General Motors vehicles this time) during Disneyland's 30th anniversary. He wrote up a plan for how it would all work and said to Ron Miller (who was in his last weeks as Disney CEO): "If we do this promotion, we'll do 12 million in attendance in 1985 and it will be a record year, two million more than we did in 1984."

Miller didn't buy it.

But Lindquist did not give up. When Eisner replaced Miller, he pitched the idea again, this time to the new CEO, but with one big caveat: "I was sitting behind Michael on an airplane headed for Orlando. Michael had only been with the company for a few weeks when I pitched the idea to him. Eisner thought the concept was ridiculous. I told him I'd make him an offer—if we don't hit 12 million in attendance by December 31, 1985, I'll resign. Eisner reconsidered and said, "Well, if you think that much of it and you're willing to put your job on the line, let's give it a try."

Lindquist's big idea, and how is was structured, is explained in the press release below that was distributed to international media in late 1984:

Disneyland Celebrates 30th Anniversary

On July 17, 1955, Disneyland welcomed its first guest. Today, three decades later, plans are underway to honor the Magic Kingdom's 250 millionth visitor and to celebrate 1985, Disneyland's magical 30th year, with the world's most festive year-long jubilee ever.

The extravagant celebration is launched on Jan. 1, 1985, with a burst of excitement as Disney characters, singers, and bands rally at the park's main entrance for the unveiling of Disneyland's "Gift-Giver Extraordinaire Machine". A computerized wonder, the specially created device will award prizes in the largest sweepstakes ever undertaken in the 30-year history of the Magic Kingdom. On that date, Disneyland's Main Gate will literally be transformed into one of the park's most exciting areas as flashing lights and whistles welcome guests who will have the opportunity to win an estimated 400,000 gifts in 1985.

Focusing on the number 30, commemorating Disneyland's anniversary, gifts will be awarded to every 30th, 300th, 3,000th, 30,000th, 300,000th, and 3,000,000th guest entering the park. Prizes range from commemorative Disneyland passports for every 30th guest to new General Motors' cars for the 30,000th, 300,000th, and 3,000,000th visitors. It is expected that an unprecedented 400 GM automobiles will be given away in the 12-month period. All of this excitement will culminate with the "Gift-Giver Extraordinaire" countdown to the luckiest prizewinner of all, Disneyland's 250 millionth guest.

Lindquist recalled, "We had to put all our park divisions to work to make this happen. It was an extraordinary measure of teamwork. First we had to computerize Disneyland's entire Main Gate that involved working with Park Operations. But all Disneyland factions including Finance, Safety, Security, Guest Services, Custodial, Parking, and more came into play. Of course, the primary driver was going to be the Marketing/Entertainment team."

The Legal division also played a large part in putting together the promotion. A big hurdle to overcome was the issue of whether Gift Giver Extraordinaire was in fact a "giveaway" and not a "raffle", an important legal distinction to make everything work on the up and up. Giveaway, by definition, is the act of giving something away free. Raffle, by definition is the act of purchasing tickets to win a prize.

The problem was that guests who bought a ticket into the park were automatically in the game...that meant it was a raffle because they purchased entry. Lindquist needed for the promotion to be a giveaway. He explained, "The way we solved that problem was by setting up a 'free' turnstile at the park's Pet Center adjacent to the Main Gate entry and one at the Disneyland Hotel. So you didn't have to buy a ticket to be eligible."

The "free" turnstile attracted many daily visitors. Lindquist continued: "Every morning there were some people who came to the park, parked their car, went to the hotel, went to the turnstile, went back to their cars, went to work, then stopped back again on the way home. We actually had three or four people win cars this way during that year."

To further lend credibility to the entire operation, Price Waterhouse (today PriceWaterhouseCoopers), the company that keeps all the Academy Award winners names secret until the Oscar broadcast, was hired to stand behind the integrity of the entire promotion.

The Gift Giver Extraordinaire wasn't the only highlight of the 30th year. There were many more offerings to market that year as described in the continuation of the Gift Giver Press Release:

> Once inside the Magic Kingdom, the birthday celebration continues with a variety of in-park entertainment to delight every member of the family. "A parade every day" is just one of the features of the 30th anniversary, along with an exciting calendar of fun-filled special themed events. Highlights of those showcased include:
>
> - The premiere of Disneyland's incomparable New Main Street Electrical Parade. After a two-year absence, this dazzling production, staged in complete darkness, returns in spring 1985 to spectacularly illuminate Main Street, U.S.A., with over a half-million sparkling and colored lights outlining its procession.
> - On Disneyland's actual 30th birth date, July 17, 1985, a 30-hour around-the-clock-and-more anniversary bash will be held. Guest bands, top-name talent, birthday parades, parties, and surprises will continue non-stop as the "happiest place on earth" welcomes guests to join in the celebration for 30 consecutive hours.
> - Galaxy [name later changed to Videopolis], an all-new high-tech dance and entertainment facility is scheduled to open at

Disneyland in summer 1985. This exciting new addition to the Magic Kingdom will give teenagers the opportunity to dance and enjoy the music of live bands in an electrifying atmosphere unlike any they've ever before experienced at the park. Included within the multi-faceted Galaxy complex will be a themed dining area and a challenging electronic video game facility.

- Marking its 30th anniversary along with Disneyland is the original *Mickey Mouse Club*. For five weekends in October/November, the entire park will be themed to that show as members of the original Mouseketeers don their ears once again and perform live, on stage, in a musical recreation of that well-remembered show. A special Mickey Mouse Club parade and rally will add to the fun.

In addition to those highlighted above, still more themed events include Disneyland's Salute to the American Hero, Springtime Fantasia, Small World Days, and the Magic Kingdom's traditional Christmas extravaganza.

All in all, Disneyland's 30th—the year of the Give Giver Extraordinaire, non-stop special events, a parade every day, more live stage shows—adds up to the biggest, best, and most ambitious 12 months in the history of the Magic Kingdom.

There was so much going on in the Park for the 30th year. However, it was the Gift-Giver Extraordinaire that drove the marketing to sky-high levels and I was right in the middle of it. (Oh, and Jack Lindquist kept his job.)

CHAPTER SEVEN

Cars, Cars, Cars

Working the PR for the 30th Anniversary surely kept all of us in Publicity incredibly busy. The Gift Giver Extraordinaire was giving away GM cars daily and publicity coverage of each winner was one of the key tenets of capturing media attention—every single day; it was marketing genius. Here's how our PR operation worked:

The Gift Giver machine was stationed at Disneyland's Main Gate. It had a constantly turning LED display that counted each person passing through an entry turnstile. Tracked by Disneyland Operations on a computer system, the machine awarded a gift to every 30th, 300th, 3,000th, 30,000th, 300,000,000th and 3,000,000th guest. Every 30,000th guest won a new GM car, and no one ever knew exactly when that was going to happen except the Operations people.

We in Publicity were notified by Operations when a 30,000th guest entry was getting close, perhaps 10–15 minutes away, although they would never tell us the exact number on the countdown clock that would set off the bells and whistles to surprise the lucky winner as they pushed through one of the Main Gate turnstiles. I was almost always part of the team to participate in the publicity routine that was carried out for every car winner, and this happened every day, sometimes twice a day depending on the park capacity. (I think on one particularly high-attendance day we even gave away three cars!)

Before heading down to the Main Gate with another publicist for the impending car giveaway, we also notified the Broadcast Services department who readied their videographer to cover the winning moment, the Disneyland photographer to capture the still images, and of course, Mickey Mouse who appeared in all the photos holding a giant ignition key featuring the word "Disneyland" and the 30th logo.

The funny thing was we'd all head down to the park's Main Gate and have to hide in the Stroller Shop to the right side of the turnstiles. We hid because many people who were Annual Passholders and could enter the park every day were on the lookout for us, because they knew when we showed up at the Main Gate that a car giveaway was near. It upped their chances to win the big prize by entering during that window of time, so we tried to keep hidden to ensure that everything was kept fair and square.

Waiting, waiting, waiting...and then confetti, bells, whistles, music, and excitement would fill the air as the winner crossed the turnstile. The Gift Giver Extraordinaire awarded yet another car! Dashing from our hideout, we would run to the winning turnstile. The video crew and still photographer would then capture the entire scene. A video producer would interview the winner, then rush to the Disneyland Broadcast Services editing bay and cut the video into a news feature that would be uplinked to a satellite and fed to the winner's hometown TV stations. A sure-fire story for local TV pick-up.

There were times, however, when things didn't go exactly as planned. Kathy Hanis, a publicist who was brought on board to help us with the 30th celebration, remembered one such incident. "I was working the Gift Giver giveaway when a Hispanic lady pushed through the turnstile and the confetti started flying and the bells and whistles began blaring. The woman was holding a 2-year-old that was very tired, and wailing. She didn't know what was going on and I tried to explain that she had just won a car. Then she said, "No habla Ingles." Crossing the turnstile right behind was the baby's mom who had purchased the winning ticket for her baby's nanny. As per the rules, a car is awarded to the person who turns the turnstile at the right time, as the nanny did, so she was the winner. The mom had but one thing to say, "My husband's going to kill me."

As with all car winners, as soon as the video crew completed their task, Mickey Mouse would arrive on the scene. We'd take Mickey, the car winner, and the still photographer to a new GM car set-up ready for us to take a staged photo. We'd have the winner in front of a new GM car with Mickey handing him or her a giant key that had the Disneyland 30th logo on it. Once that was done, the photographer had to quickly develop the film (remember film?) so that Publicity could select the best shot from which an 8x10 black-and-white print could be made and sent overnight by Fedex (no email or digital files!) to the winner's hometown newspapers along with a personalized press release.

To back that up, we'd also call the newspaper's news desks and let them know about the win and the materials being sent, as well as offering them an on-the-spot interview with the winner. Often, a phone interview immediately took place. We also pitched the interview to the local radio stations in that town and again, the winner did the interviews "live". The winners were ultimately able to select a GM car of their choice that was delivered to their local dealerships for pickup.

This went on every day, and as cited previously, sometimes twice a day. Disneyland's 30th anniversary got incredible, daily, publicity coverage—hometown by hometown. Marketing magic, if you will. I had a map of the United States in my office with pins indicating every winner's city. By the end of the 30th year, the map was almost totally covered in pins. Ultimately, 406 cars were given away that year. Of course, all of this was in addition to getting publicity out about every other activity going on for the 30th year. To launch the Gift Giver Extraordinaire and all of the 30th anniversary festivities, we held a massive press event.

When I say "massive" press event, that's exactly what I mean. We didn't just invite a sampling of media from all over the country, we invited press from all over the world to be Disneyland's guest for a few days. Literally hundreds of media were exposed to all the goings-on for the 30th. And they arrived en masse. Numerous radio stations broadcast "live" from the park, stationed in strategic locations throughout Disneyland.

TV crews from news stations all over the country were provided everything they needed to put together great stories, from Disneyland Publicity arranging interviews with park executives, Disney celebrities, and Disney characters, to shooting video on attractions and arranging special setups. Still photographers from news agencies all over the world were also catered to so that they got the shot, whatever it was (within reason, of course).

The Publicity Department led the charge in making all the arrangements needed for any media person. Since the PR staff was relatively small, we recruited people from all areas of Marketing to work with us so that every press representative was handled on a one-to-one personal basis. Tim O'Day, a long-time Disney Promotions and Marketing executive, worked tirelessly with us to set up many of those interviews and to make sure everything ran smoothly. There were times, however, when he encountered little bumps in the road, especially with rock-and-roll radio DJs who were often unpredictable. O'Day recalled, "We were often requested to have the Disney princesses do live, on-air interviews and most of the interviewers were respectful of the characters, their origin stories, and personalities. However, some of the "shock jocks" would sometimes ask Snow White for her phone number and what she was doing Saturday night. This was obviously frowned upon because it took the listener out of the Disneyland experience. The Seven Dwarfs weren't very happy about it, either."

O'Day's background with radio and TV remotes led him to develop a great marketing tool called the Disneyland Media Guide which "contained historical background on the park, lots of fun trivia, and interesting facts that DJs could use on the air". Most importantly, it also included appropriate questions for such characters as Snow White, Mary Poppins, Cinderella, and the others that could be interviewed.

The Media Guide as developed by O'Day became so successful it was also adapted for use at the 1991 Walt Disney World Resort 20th anniversary media kick-off (and for many Disneyland and Walt Disney World media events for years to come). It was also adapted and translated into numerous languages for use during the 1992 grand opening of Disneyland Paris (then called Euro Disney). A valuable publicity tool, the guide has been revised and re-shaped through the years and utilized for the opening of Disney parks and events well into the 21st century.

All media at the various celebratory events were immersed in the totality of the Disney resorts. Not only were they invited to work the goings-on, but to have fun at what were often extravagant parties and activities. I remember three Disneyland campaigns that were very different than the typical anniversary commemorations. They were Circus Fantasy, State Fair, and Blast to the Past, all of which were presented in the mid-1980s.

O'Day, who worked the marketing and promotional angle (along with the PR staff) for all three promotional campaigns, explained that they were not equally successful. "These were multi-month seasonal events created to boost attendance at different times of the year. It was an odd fit to have a circus-themed event within Disneyland, especially one that featured something called "The Globe of Death" stationed in front Sleeping Beauty Castle!"

O'Day recalled another "Circus Fantasy" odd fit: "At regular intervals during the day a human was shot out of a cannon, flying through the air from one end of Main Street to the other—a truly peculiar sight, even for Disneyland!"

I do, however, remember a fun aspect of Circus Fantasy that was concocted by the Publicity Department. We actually set up a clown school in one of the backstage areas for TV hosts doing stories from the park. We brought in specialists who taught them how to juggle, take a pie in the face, and apply clown makeup. It kept the circus theme in the forefront when it was time for them to "report" live from the park.

O'Day said, "State Fair was a terrific late summer/early fall event overlaid to the park. We had pig races that were extremely fun and popular, logrollers out on the Rivers of America, carnival games placed around Town Square, and a Ferris wheel in front of the Main Street Train Station. With the typical southern California Indian summers, it was a perfect overlay for that time of year."

Themed foods were also available around the park, including corn on the cob and barbecued turkey legs (this was long before they became a staple of the menu at Disney parks).

Disneyland broadcast producer Tony Perri created an award-winning video news story on the pig races. To accommodate the competitions and provide gallery seating for Disneyland guests, the pot-bellied pigs raced around a specially built track housed under a huge red-and-white striped tent. In the video, Perri's voiceover excitedly calls the race much like it was a horse race as footage focuses on the running pigs with camera shots angled at pig level while the words "Pig Cam" flashed on the screen.

At the freeze-frame finish of the race, Perri, in voiceover, draws on-screen circles and lines from this pig to that, pointing out the strategies of the winning swine as a sportscaster might illustrate a winning football play. Bob Roth, who was the Disneyland Publicity Manager at the time, provided Perri with the video's closing line: "Won by a snout." It was hilarious. You can view it on YouTube here: youtu.be/Ee82HuAO4yM.

The State Fair event also had a daily hometown marketing ploy built in, much like the car giveaways for Disneyland's 30th. This concept was to invite the beauty queen (Miss Alabama, Miss Kansas, Miss Ohio, etc.) for each of the 50 states, one day at a time, to the State Fair celebration, videotape her fun day at Disneyland, cut together a story, and feed it via broadcast satellite to her hometown TV news stations that same day. The daily procedure generated Disneyland media coverage for fifty straight days. It culminated with the arrival of Miss America. The result was sure-fire TV pickup featuring each of the local beauty queens, and a great national press story starring Miss America.

The most popular of the three seasonal events was Blast to the Past, showcased for several months in 1988 and 1989. O'Day said, "The great thing about Blast to the Past was that it was built off the fun and nostalgia of the 1950s, a trend that was popular in the 1970s and 80s with TV shows and movies like *Happy Days, American Graffiti, Grease, Back to the Future*, and *Peggy Sue Got Married*. The event was phenomenally successful, mostly because of one of the most infectious shows Disneyland has ever produced: the Main Street Hop."

This rock 'n rollin,' over-the-top street spectacular was the brainchild of Disney Creative Entertainment Director Marilyn Magness, who has produced hundreds of shows inside and outside of Disney, including Super Bowl Halftime extravaganzas, Radio City Music Hall spectaculars, and presidential inaugurals, among others. The Main Street Hop was an immediate crowd-pleaser. Magness recalled, "The entire length of Main Street, U.S.A. was used as a stage. The focal points were three gigantic juke boxes set in place along the street with Elvis impersonators and rock 'n roll dancers on top. More girl and boy singers and dancers, costumed in poodle skirts and letterman sweaters, interacted and revved up the crowd lining both sides of the street."

A classic 1950s and early 60s soundtrack loudly reverberated from the Disneyland sound system as the crowd got into the spirit of things. Then, at a given point in the musical spectacle, hundreds of hula-hoops were sent sliding down ropes from the rooftops of Main Street to the performers below. They began hula-hooping and brought parade watchers into the show itself to do so as well.

Toward the end of the high-spirited production, as the Beach Boys hit song "Little Honda" played, the sound of engine-revving motorbikes was heard. A long line of riders on white Honda motor scooters emerged from Disneyland's backstage area riding a loop down one end of Main Street and up the other side. As the combination of music, dancing, hula hooping, and motor scooters reached its height, a finale confetti blast reigned down from the rooftops of Main Street, U.S.A.

The doo-wop fun of this "Streetacular" also inspired a media event that captured worldwide press attention. Called "The Super Duper Hula-Hooper" and featuring the king of "The Twist", recording artist Chubby Checker, it was staged in front of Sleeping Beauty Castle. The idea was to break the world record for people hula hooping in one place at the same time. Checker sang his hit song "Let's Twist Again" while leading 1,527 people in what became the largest hula-hoop gathering ever.

CHAPTER EIGHT

Welcome, President Reagan

The Walt Disney World marketing team came up with a bold idea to "wow" the newly installed Eisner and Wells. It involved the sitting U.S. president at the time, Ronald Reagan. Having been elected for his second term, Reagan's swearing-in ceremony held on January 21, 1985, and traditionally held outdoors, had to be moved inside because of bone-chilling temperatures that Washington, D.C. experienced that day. All of the outdoor events scheduled, including over 50 high school bands from around the country that had traveled to the nation's capital to march in the inaugural parade, were cancelled.

Enter the marketing team in Orlando with an idea to turn a big weather disappointment into a once-in-a-lifetime promotional opportunity. Phil Lengyel, then vice president of Marketing for Walt Disney World explained, "We were looking for more ways to promote EPCOT Center that had opened just a few years earlier. The idea was to invite the president to restage the inauguration and we'd do it at EPCOT in May when the weather is great, the park attendance isn't as great, and we'll invite all the high school bands that didn't get a chance to perform for Reagan in D.C. to have a second chance. Of course, for the first time, we'd get a sitting U.S. president to make a visit to a Disney theme park."

Lengyel and his boss, Walt Disney World marketing chief Tom Elrod, whom the Orlando Sentinel once called "a marketing whiz", and Disney Parks marketing guru Jack Lindquist, referred to as "one of the most outstanding marketing people in the world", decided to pursue the idea by themselves without telling anyone else or getting any approval from their bosses in Burbank. They were flying by the seat of their pants.

Pulling Disney company strings, the marketing duo found their way to Ronald Reagan's chief of staff, Michael Deaver. Lengyel recalled, "Elrod and I flew to D.C. to meet with Deaver and pitched him the idea. Deaver responded with unexpected immediacy: "I'm going to see the President in a little while," he said. "Why don't you guys stick around and I'll get you an answer real quick." We waited. Before long, Deaver returned and said, "Okay, we'll do it." I'll never forget it. Elrod and I sat there and looked at each other and said, "What are we going to do now?"

The marketing duo hadn't asked anybody in the company if they could do this, an event that would no doubt make quite a dent in the Walt Disney World Resort marketing budget and be a logistical nightmare to stage. Dick Nunis, who was then head of Walt Disney Parks and Resorts, didn't know, and certainly the relatively newly installed Eisner and Wells didn't know.

But who could turn down an opportunity to host the sitting president of the United States and all the media coverage that would come with it? Certainly not the hierarchy at the Disney Company. President Reagan even had a history with Disney. He had served as one of the hosts, along with Walt Disney and TV personalities Art Linkletter and Bob Cummings, of the live television special that broadcast the opening of Disneyland in 1955. But putting together all the theme park factions needed to pull off Reagan's appearance at EPCOT Center would be quite a task. Lengyel explained, "It was a matter of organizing the event and then getting the Disney machine behind it. We got the entire marketing group together— Publicity, Promotions, Public Relations, Advertising, Creative Services, Special Events, Corporate Alliances—to get them in lockstep moving forward. We were one group with different functioning elements. We created what the idea needed to be, but it was up to each specific area to figure out how we would accomplish it from their perspective."

And the marketing group was only the tip of the iceberg when it came to coordinating such an extravaganza.

Ultimately, "The President's Inaugural Band Parade," titled to focus on the student bands that never got to perform at the D.C. event, impacted nearly every division of the Disney outpost in Orlando: "We thought about things like community implications so we got Community Relations involved, all things had to be coordinated so we had to be in sync with Operations, we needed Transportation to handle moving people from one place to another, the Food folks had to feed hundreds of people, hotel personnel had to be included, Security of course was heavily involved working with the Secret Service, after all it was the sitting president of the United States who was going to be our special guest."

Most importantly, Lengyel insisted that everyone be in it from the beginning because the ideas from the different factions were, as he stated: "As valuable as ours. I never wanted any of them just taking an order from the marketing group. They each had an absolute interest in making our events successful, and, quite frankly, they were the pros, we were just the dreamers."

The President's Inaugural Band Parade was presented on Memorial Day Monday, May 27, 1985. A number of the original high school bands that were to march in the D.C. parade attended to march in the EPCOT Center procession. Orlando's Osceola County served as the official sponsor of the event and helped to defray the transportation costs of over 2,500 student musicians from the 16 states that took part.

President Reagan and his wife, Nancy, arrived at EPCOT via Marine One helicopter and, after a brief meeting with Disney officials and Florida politicians, soon arrived at a specially built reviewing stand across from The American Adventure, the Colonial-style host pavilion inside EPCOT Center's World Showcase that takes audiences on a journey through American history. Reagan was introduced by Disney CEO, Michael Eisner with remarks that included: "I was in Washington 105 degrees ago. It was minus 20 degrees at the Inauguration and it's 85 here today. Even though this isn't the official inaugural parade, it's the first time since 1789 that it's not been in Washington. I just want to say that, if Walt Disney were alive today, he'd be proud to be standing where I am, with the president of the United States."

Reagan stepped up to the podium and made a short speech on his visit that paid tribute to the student musicians who got a second chance at glory: "Well, indeed it is an honor for me to be here today to receive a magnificent gift on a second, warmer Inauguration Day. I understand that in preparing for this event more than 2,500 young people worked with sponsors in the private sector who donated food, transportation, and lodging. And each of you who helped to make this private sector initiative possible has my heartfelt thanks."

With President and Mrs. Reagan seated in the reviewing stand along with Michael Eisner; his wife, Jane; and a host of VIPs including Walt Disney's wife, Lillian, the long-awaited procession that never was happened under a sunny Florida sky. Led by Mickey Mouse costumed in stars and strips, the parade got underway and followed a 1.3 mile route around EPCOT's World Showcase Lagoon. It was followed by a spectacular daytime fireworks display, a fifteen thousand balloon release, and a flyover by four F16 fighter jets. A good time was had by all. And importantly, by Eisner's estimate, EPCOT Center received $100 million of free publicity that day.

Thank you Tom Elrod and Phil Lengyel...and President Reagan, too.

CHAPTER NINE

Lindquist Strikes Again

The year 1987 brought another marketing bonanza to the Disneyland Publicity Department, albeit one of a much smaller, but no less covered, genius idea called Disney Dollars. Again, Jack Lindquist devised the concept. He explained, "Disneyland has long been considered its own nation. If you count guests and cast members, we have a population in the millions. In keeping with that theme, it seemed natural to create our own currency. It's an extension of the fantasy environment we offer our guests."

The idea came to Jack as he was flying back to L.A. from Europe. "I had eleven hours with nothing to do so I thought I'd work on my expense report. I had a bunch of different envelopes with various currencies. There were French francs, English pounds, and German deutsch marks. I thought about Disneyland being a place where people visit from all over the world, so why don't we have our own currency??

When Jack got back to his office, he shared the idea with the Disneyland marketing staff. They thought it was a good promotional idea, but that was not what Lindquist was thinking. "I told them that the mindset was not promotional, Disney Dollars had to be real currency, the realm of the kingdom. I got the go-ahead from Michael and Frank and we were off."

Disney Dollars were launched at Disneyland on May 5, 1987. I handled the PR for this project and remember it well. It was a marketing venture that exemplified how Disney always goes the extra mile. As Lindquist had insisted, no cheap promotional "Monopoly" money for this concept. The production of Disney Dollars employed highly sophisticated techniques that incorporated real-world currency anti-counterfeiting measures. Each bill carried an individual serial number, and to further prevent forgeries, the bills were printed on expensive rag cotton stock that bore a subtle watermark, second only to U.S. currency stock. State-of-the-art four-color printing for Disney Dollars was handled by Embossing Printers, Inc.

Initially, Disney Dollars were produced in just two denominations—$1 and $5—and each bill was to be equal one-to-one with U.S. dollars. They were designed in full color and were the same physical size (6¼" x 2¾") as U.S. paper currency for ease of handling. Mickey Mouse appeared on the face of the $1 bill with Sleeping Beauty Castle on the reverse side, and Goofy was showcased on the face of $5 with the *Mark Twain* Riverboat on the reverse.

The finishing touch of the imagery was the signature of Scrooge McDuck, Secretary of the Disney Treasury, on the face of the bills. The artwork, the vision of Anne White, Disneyland's Creative Services Manager, was stunning. The printing process, however, was just the first part of the overall course in creating the most realistic currency possible.

The next step in producing Disney Dollars was a complex intaglio engraving procedure. This gave the bills raised texture and fine detail, mirroring the printing techniques used for U.S. currency. After the bills were printed by Embossing Printers, they were then shipped to Chicago, where the United States Banknote Corporation (a recognized leader in the design of stock certificates, bank notes, bonds, and other security documents) completed the engraving process.

For the 1987 inaugural run, over $2 million of Disney Dollars were put into circulation at Disneyland and were an instant success. Guests could receive their change in Disney Dollars for ticket purchases or for any regular transactions throughout the park, such as food, merchandise, and services. Then, after a day at Disneyland, the currency could be changed back into U.S. notes. But many of the beautiful, brightly colored bills were instead tucked away as souvenirs. According to Lindquist, over the years bills that were never used totaled over $125 million, although those notes can still be used as Disney currency at any time.

Just five months after the highly successful launch, in October 1987, Disney Dollars were put into circulation at Walt Disney World, as well. In November 1989, a $10 note bearing the image of Minnie Mouse was added, becoming the first paper currency in the United States to bear the portrait of a female. Park guests were advised to not be surprised if someone posed the question, "Do you have five Mickeys for a Goofy?"

Of course, Disney Dollars didn't just quietly appear at Disneyland; they were launched with a splashy PR event to introduce the new currency to the world. Media, of course, were invited to witness the arrival of the first Disney Dollars to Disneyland.

As they gathered photo-ready at the park's entrance, an actual Brink's armored truck arrived with a police escort, sirens blaring. The doors at the back of the truck were opened and there stood Scrooge McDuck holding two Disney Dollar moneybags in his hand. He jumped out of the back of the truck waving around his "cash stash" while the photographers clicked away. Mission accomplished.

As an aside on Disney Dollars, Lindquist remembered an interesting story about the currency. "I got a call from Kellogg's who were interested in putting Disney Dollars in every box of their corn flakes. I thought it was a very interesting idea and invited them out to California to talk about it. When we met they told me they were thinking about putting one Disney Dollar in about 1.5 million boxes a month. I thought that was a sensational idea. Then they said, 'What is the discount?' I said there is no discount. They said, 'You can't be serious.' I said, 'I'll tell you what. You go to the U.S. Treasury and tell them you'll put $1.5 million, one dollar at a time, in every box of corn flakes and I'll give you the same discount they do.' I never heard from them again!"

By 1986, Michael Eisner and Frank Wells were well into creating concepts to revitalize Disneyland. According to Jim Hill, a Disney fan and occasional blogger for *The Huffington Post*, Eisner wanted to come up with something that he could show to filmmaker George Lucas and the King of Pop, Michael Jackson, who loved Disneyland and was a frequent visitor. Eisner was thinking about a new 3D movie for the parks and wanted Disney Imagineers to collaborate with Lucas and Jackson. The collaboration resulted in a 17-minute 3D film that was directed by Hollywood film director, Francis Ford Coppola and starred Academy Award-winning actress Angelica Houston, titled *Captain EO*.

The 3D film debuted at Disneyland at the 700-seat Magic Eye Theater in Tomorrowland on September 18, 1986. Each attendee was given a pair of plastic 3D glasses for viewing. The opening was a giant media event, as big or bigger than a full-blown Hollywood premiere. There were more than 200 members from the international press who attended. They were each given a press kit containing nine separate releases, six photos, and a commemorative *Captain EO* T-shirt. A *Captain EO* video press kit was also prepared for TV media.

Wall-to-wall celebrities and their families were invited and 125 of them attended. At 2 pm that day, in weather that approached nearly 100 degrees, a parade of celebrities in various vehicles made its way down Main Street, U.S.A. to Tomorrowland, waving to the Disneyland guests who had lined up five-deep to catch a glimpse of their favorite stars.

Catherine Bach, Elizabeth Montgomery, Alan Thicke, Erik Estrada, John Ritter, Lisa Hartman, Whoopi Goldberg, Charles Bronson, LaToya Jackson, Janet Jackson, Sissy Spacek, Rosemary Clooney, Dr. Joyce Brothers, Debra Winger, Annette Funicello, Elliot Gould, Dolph Lundgren, and even Jack Nicholson, who rode with his then girlfriend, Angelica Huston, down Main Street in an antique car waving to cheering fans. One special person did not attend—Michael Jackson—although rumors abounded that he was there in disguise.

Following the success of *Captain EO*, Lucas embarked on another collaboration with Disney called Star Tours, a motion-simulator attraction based on Lucas' phenomenally successful *Star Wars* film series. The opening day event was held on January 9, 1987. Michael Eisner and George Lucas were on hand to open the attraction, along with *Star Wars*/Star Tours characters C-3PO and R2-D2.

The cost of the new attraction came in at $32 million, almost twice the cost of building all of Disneyland in 1955. The innovative new ride opened to throngs of guests, and of course, throngs of press. There were hundreds of media eager for press releases, photos, interviews, video clips, canned Disney PR -produced TV news and radio stories, and more.

When the attraction opened, Star Tours press kits were released to the media. They each contained stories on George Lucas, Michael Eisner, and C-3PO. An additional electronic press kit offered an hour of video, with a large part of it devoted to the attraction's elaborate grand opening ceremony featuring actor Anthony Daniels as C3PO and assorted actors dressed as Luke, Han, Leia, Chewbacca, and Darth Vader dancing and acting out several scenes from the *Star Wars* films.

There was also a TV special that aired around the time of the opening of the ride. The program, *A Vacation in Space*, was designed to promote the attraction by looking at how Star Tours was made, as well as the history of space travel and space-related films. Some highlights of the program included segments on C-3PO and R2-D2 and the attraction's vehicle called the StarSpeeder 3000.

As part of the Star Tours experience, upon exiting the attraction riders were led directly into a store called Star Trader that sold merchandise based on *Star Wars*, including action figures, clothing, and other items. The store also sold exclusive merchandise available only at Disney theme parks, including action figures of the various droids seen in the ride and queue, and StarSpeeder 3000 toys.

Two more special guests were also invited to participate in the Star Tours opening: Dick Rutan and Jeana Yeager. Just weeks earlier they had completed an epic and history-making journey as the first pilots to ever fly around the world non-stop without refueling. For nine days they flew in Rutan's light aircraft, *Voyager*. The two pilots battled fatigue, privacy, turbulence, and storms while living in a cockpit 3–5 feet wide by 7 feet long as they circled the globe. The flight covered 26,358 miles. The story generated huge front-page headlines at the time.

On the evening of the opening, Michael Eisner and his wife invited Rutan and Yaeger to have dinner with them at Disneyland's Plaza Inn on Main Street, U.S.A. During the meal, Eisner's wife, Jane, asked Rutan and Yeager what they were going to do now that they'd achieved this momentous milestone. Yaeger responded, "Well, we're going to Disneyland!"

Jane thought that such a great reply might make a fantastic slogan in an advertising campaign and suggested it to her husband. He liked it and the rest, as they say, is history.

The incredibly successful "What's Next" (titled by Disney) marketing campaign was all about getting TV commercials on the air within hours of a big win or moment, mostly in sports when the star of the game answers a simple question posed by an unseen narrator: "Now that you've won the Super Bowl (for example), what are you going to do next?" In their moment of absolute triumph, they reply, "I'm going to Disneyland (or Disney World; two versions of the ads were always provided to run on both the east and the west coasts to serve both parks). Viewers were amazed, but getting the footage and then getting it edited and on the air within a few hours was no easy task.

CHAPTER TEN

What's Next?

Immediately after that fateful dinner, Michael Eisner got his wife's idea rolling. Dave Lancashire, a Disneyland staff producer, recalled, "I think it was literally the next day that there was a conference call that I was a part of. The call was from Eisner who had Disneyland and Walt Disney World marketing executives on the line. He said he had a big idea and he wanted people thinking about it fast."

Once everybody understood the concept, a list of upcoming major world sports and non-sports events were compiled. Lancashire explained, "The key to all of it was that Michael liked the immediacy of it...that this big thing has happened and the next thing on the person's mind was going to Disneyland or Walt Disney World to celebrate."

Michael teamed up with Tom Elrod at Walt Disney World to spearhead the "What's Next?" campaign. "The chain of command on all the spots was Michael, Tom, and whoever was producing the spot," added Lancashire. Ultimately, production was handled either by the West Coast team at Disneyland or the East Coast team at Disney World, whichever was most appropriate at the time.

It was decided that the first TV spot was to be shot at Super Bowl XXI on January 25, 1987. This was less than two weeks after Jane Eisner originated the concept. Lancashire said, "We had to quickly decide how all of this was going to be approached. We discussed working in conjunction with NFL Films because they would already be on the field shooting the game along with a Disney crew. Then, of course, the Disney folks would need all-access passes to be able to access the field, the locker room, and anywhere else we might need to be without knowing what was going to happen in advance."

That year, recalled Lancashire, the Super Bowl was to be played in Disneyland's back yard, just 35 miles north of Anaheim at the Rose Bowl in Pasadena, California: "Unfortunately, our advertising manager happened to be going out of town that weekend, so the folks at Walt Disney World came out and shot it on film. It was decided to get the 'I'm going to

Disneyland' and 'I'm going to Disney World' line from whoever ended up being the most valuable player in the game. Our guess was that it would most likely be the winning team's quarterback, and we were right: Phil Simms, quarterback of the New York Giants, was named MVP. He was our the first guinea pig."

The game footage used was shot by NFL Films and the famous "line" was shot by the Disney crew out in the middle of field at the end of the game. When the TV spot aired, it was an instant hit. However, according to Lancashire, Eisner and Elrod were not totally satisfied: "For that first spot, everything was shot on 16mm film because that's how the NFL did their coverage back then. Then they had to send the film to New Jersey for processing and then have it sent back to be edited. Because of all that, the first spot had a several day lag before it aired. While the spot itself was a great success, per Michael and Tom, we had to figure out a way to get it on the air faster."

The first thing the Disneyland and Disney World teams decided was to move from film to video to shoot the ads. "Using video, we were able to edit immediately after getting the footage," said Lancashire. "We would make editing facility arrangements in advance in whatever city we were going to be in and they'd be ready for us. Then we'd have to set up a satellite feed a few hours later to be able to uplink the edited footage and make it available to TV stations around the country to downlink. We worked with our media partners who worked with the networks to quickly get the spot on the air."

But, continued Lancashire, getting the footage was quite a feat. "That was the thing...the challenge at the end of the game. I'm a sports fan and being on the field of the Super Bowl or the World Series at the moment the game is won is just so exhilarating. But I was working, too, and I had to make sure we were getting what we needed."

As the game neared the end, it became crunch time. "In some cases, it was easy. But sometimes you're just out in the middle of it with all the pushing and shoving and just trying to get in there to the person you need to reach to get the lines on video."

Once they got what they needed, the crew would literally run out of the venue to their cars as fast as they could. In the process they had to gather up all their tapes and get the game footage from any other non-Disney crews who were shooting for them and head for the editing facility. Sometimes they had as many as six crews shooting the game, and time was of the essence. Lancashire recalled, "With the World Series, we had several games from which to choose footage not always just using footage from the final game. Capturing great moments from several games brought scope and context to the final spot. It required more work, more communication, and more teamwork. But that was never an obstacle; the idea was to create the best spot in a limited amount of time."

Getting the spot on the air also required up-front work. "We had to buy the air time prior to game day making our best guess as to what time the networks would have the final spot. And we'd have to have a back-up spot ready just in case we didn't make it in time," Lancashire explained. "It was a lot of solid coordination and communication with the network and stations to let them know when they could expect to get it. But everyone was having as much fun as we were because they'd see these spots come down on satellite, or it was hand-delivered in some cases, and they knew there was an immediacy to get it on. After that first year, it just got faster and faster."

Walt Disney World's team produced the first two "What's Next?" spots, the first being Super Bowl XXI and the second, flying to Australia in February 1987 to get the line from Dennis Connor, winner of sailing's big championship, the America's Cup Race.

As the first year moved forward, Lancashire and the Disneyland team jumped into the fray, eventually covering twelve of the "What's Next?" spots during Lancashire's tenure at the park. Walt Disney World was there when it started, but eventually producing the spots was split between the two Disney parks.

In preparation for shooting, Lancashire had to make contact with the people who were the most likely to answer the question, "What are you doing next?" He said, "We'd meet with whomever we thought were the best candidates for the ad a day or two before the shoot. It was very challenging to try to get ten minutes with any of the players to explain exactly what we were going to do."

Consequently, Lancashire and his team would spend a lot of time sitting in hotel lobbies waiting to catch them coming or going. The hope was that the player's agents, who had been told about the TV spot, had spoken to their clients so that Lancashire's few minutes with them did not come as a total surprise. He said, "We never had set appointments with anyone, it was all very loose. Since it was always catch-as-catch-can, there were a few unusual meetings. One time, myself and our business affairs person, Joyce Trent-Morgan, met with Jim Kelly, a quarterback with the Buffalo Bills, in his hotel while he was on the bed watching television in his underwear! It was all an adrenalin rush because everything we did was kind of by the seat of our pants."

According to Lancashire, the legal side of getting things set up was also an important factor in getting the spot delivered. "All the contracts with the players were contingent upon 'if you get chosen'. Joyce was our business affairs person and would handle getting all the clearance contracts with whatever league we were dealing with."

Many important factors fell under the heading "clearance contract", including rights to use footage and any fees associated with that footage. Also to be covered was anything having to do with being able to use marks and logos like the Olympic Rings and team insignias for which there was generally a rights fee and a usage fee associated with the footage that was shot.

A few days before the event to be covered, Joyce or the business affairs person from Walt Disney World would fly to the city where the upcoming game was to be held. Then they would work through the player's agents and hook up with the player candidates through whatever means and get their signatures on the contracts.

Getting properly credentialed was another important factor in the mix, albeit a bit less "on the fly" as most other aspects of putting it all together. Lancashire explained, "That would be handled in advance through the various leagues. Generally, we had all-access credentials that included the field of play, locker room, whatever we needed to get the job done. Overall, it was pretty high stress. You had to get the best footage possible and then go edit. The reality is that you can edit the piece a thousand different ways, but the main thing is that you always had to tell the story by telling it with the highs and lows. The angst, the joy, everything that went into that game or series for that athlete had to be communicated."

The music that accompanied the spot's visuals was Disney's Oscar-winning anthem "When You Wish Upon a Star" from the classic animated film *Pinocchio*. The lyrics played an important role in telling the story and in which direction to go with the editing. "We had to pair the visuals with those lyrics. 'When you wish upon a star, makes no difference who you are, anything your heart desires will come to you,' are great words to work with. 'Anything your heart desires' was always paired with a great emotional moment. 'Will come to you' was always the moment of celebration. There were great touch points that really made it work."

When the spots were completed, they needed to be approved before airing, if possible. Lancashire said, "The spots basically had three major links. Michael, Tom Elrod, and whoever was producing the spot. If it was me, I was talking to Tom who was talking to Michael. That was after the event when the spot was completed and we needed to get final approval from them to air it."

But getting that approval also had its speed bumps. "Sometimes it might be the middle of the night when we finished editing and there was really not enough time to satellite feed it for approvals. Remember, this was pre-internet and you couldn't just send someone a digital file. You had to send it via satellite where someone could take it down on the other side and deliver it to someone's home. It just took too much time. Oftentimes, we just worked with our best instincts as to how the spot worked and then just got it on the air."

However, even though it might be after the fact, Eisner and Elrod still had input. "They would see the spot when it was broadcast and if they had any issues with it we would re-edit and do a second satellite feed with the revised piece," said Lancashire. "But most of the time, they loved what we or the Walt Disney World team put together and it was used as is."

Eventually, the turnaround time from end-of-game to being broadcast on-air was reduced to just a few hours as time went on, but Lancashire remembered the fastest spot his team ever produced, getting it on air within ten minutes of the end of a game: "It was the final 1999 Women's World Cup Soccer game held at the Rose Bowl in Pasadena with over 90,000 in attendance. It was a triumph because the United States Women's Team won."

The extra advantage that Lancashire had for this game was that by 1999 Disney owned ABC and ESPN, having acquired them in 1996, and they were the host broadcasters of the game. "Because I got to sit in the broadcast truck and was able to watch the game from there, at half-time we actually started to cut the piece together. Then, at the commercials, we'd assemble more and more, and it got to the point where we had seventeen or eighteen seconds and all that was missing was the winning moment and celebration. That particular game went into overtime, and when it did I told the guys in the truck what I was planning to do and rushed out to the field to get what was the winning kick for the U.S. team and the celebratory footage. We got the entire women's team together and had them all yell, 'I'm going to Disneyland', and then, of course, 'I'm going to Disney World.'

Perfect.

Back in the truck, Lancashire and his team quickly got the winning footage incorporated into the already pre-edited spot. With amazing luck, it happened that ABC had a network promo coming up just minutes following the end of the game: "They allowed us to use that time to put our just-completed commercial for both east and west coast versions, and we were on the air within ten minutes of the end of the game!"

For the record, most of the athletes and others who have uttered the famous line really do go to Disneyland or Disney World shortly after doing the spot for which they are paid handsomely, in the vicinity of $100,000, although most monies were donated to charity.

Disney provides an all-expense paid trip, flying them and their family to Disneyland or Walt Disney World Resorts and welcoming them with a beautiful hotel suite for the duration of their stay. They are also made the grand marshal of a Magic Kingdom parade and take part in various events for Disney during their time at the parks.

Disney's "What's Next?" TV spots were incredibly successful and continue to be produced to this day (although much more sparingly), nearly three decades from the first airing. It was an exceptional marketing idea that came from the CEO's wife. Lancashire concluded, "Everyone knew how great this idea was right from the beginning. And everybody was always interested in how we pulled it off back in the day with no internet, no digital files, little use of cell phone technology...nothing. It was pretty phenomenal."

Still is.

CHAPTER ELEVEN

Mickey Celebrates His 60th

A key corporate anniversary celebration in 1988 was Mickey's 60th birthday. It proved to be another PR bonanza that was commemorated throughout the company, particularly via the theme parks. It was indeed one of Disney's first priority synergy projects that emanated, at the time, from the company's Corporate Marketing Department that was later to become Corporate Synergy and Special Projects headed by a young executive named Art Levitt. I was very involved from the Disneyland standpoint.

Jack Lindquist, not surprisingly, came up with something truly out of left field—one of the biggest (literally) ideas within Mickey's 60th campaign—a wacky notion called Mickey in the Cornfield. While he devised the concept, it took a great deal of assistance from park staff and outside entities to bring the idea to fruition. I might add that creative marketing ideas for the parks emanated from many talented executives in all marketing disciplines; however, when it came to BIG ideas, so many of them began with Lindquist, at least the ones I remember best.

This idea also came to Jack on an airplane. "I was flying over Texas on my way back to L.A. from Orlando. I was peering out the window and could see circles on the ground created by Texas' natural gas fields. I got to thinking that if you take one big circle and then two little ones, you've got Mickey Mouse!"

Jack's mind then jumped to the feasibility of creating a Mickey profile large enough to be seen from 35,000 feet in the air. "When I got back to California we talked about it, but nobody seemed excited. The big question was, "How much is it going to cost?" I thought it wouldn't be that expensive, so they appeased me and said, "Sure, go ahead, but don't take a lot of time and don't spend a lot of money."

After researching the possibilities, it was determined that an Iowa cornfield would provide the best color contrasts to see a Mickey from the air.

At that point, Lindquist passed the concept to off to Mimi Schaaf in the Marketing Department and had her fly to Iowa and meet with staff from the University of Iowa's Agriculture Department to find out if they could help make Mickey happen. Lindquist explained, "As it turned out we lucked out, it was the 100th anniversary of the school and they were looking for something to do to get some attention."

The agricultural folks told Schaff that at least a square mile of land was going to be needed if Mickey was going to be able to be seen from 35,000 feet, and then they put her in touch with several farmers in the area. Ultimately, the farming Pitzenberger family of Sheffield, Iowa (population 1,224), working in conjunction with the University of Iowa's Agricultural Department, was selected to showcase what became Mickey in the Cornfield.

A July 1988 Associated Press piece recounts the story:

> Last fall, as Mickey's 60th birthday approached, the Disney organiza-tion began working in Iowa to locate a field to plant in the shape of his head, preferably one beneath a well-traveled route of commercial airliners. With the help of Iowa State University, searchers found a farm that fit the bill, property rented by Richard Pitzenberger and his sons Joe, Ted, and Rick.
>
> Using a design developed with the help of a surveyor, Joe Pitzenberger planted corn in the shape of Mickey's head surrounded by oats in a day and a half last spring. He said it took just three hours longer than usual to plant the field, which has been kept alive by rain that has eluded some other areas of the state.
>
> The design consists of 6.5 million corn plants surrounded by 300 acres of oats, and it's 1.1 miles from the tip of Mickey's nose to the end of his ear. "It's been great," said Joe Pitzenberger of the attention his work has achieved, although he admits that the famous field mouse also is making the Pitzenbergers' the butt of some good-natured jokes around town. "Mickey Mouse operation is the one we hear the most," said Pitzenberger. "I tell 'em I've heard it before."

Needless to say, the "Mickey Mouse operation" generated worldwide media attention and the real Mickey along with Minnie, Donald, and Goofy all attended the media event in Sheffield, Iowa, that celebrated the unique 60th birthday portrait. *Earforce One*, a Mickey-shaped hot-air balloon, soared in the Iowa sky while 15,000 people came to celebrate the event. Of course, Disney staff coordinated with all the airlines that flew routes over Mickey to alert passengers to the planted cornfield as they passed over.

The attention generated by Mickey in the Cornfield not only created enor-mous media coverage, but generated a new revenue stream for the small town in which it was planted. "The local crop dusters would take people up in their planes for $5 a pop to fly over the cornfield," said Lindquist.

But planting the field later presented a problem: what to do with the actual corn that grew. Lindquist recalled, "We talked to the local Chamber of Commerce and told them they could have the corn but they said, "What can we do with it?" I told them: "Maybe you can bottle it, put a label on it, and sell it as Cornfield Mickey and make some money."

The Chamber did just that and sold 20,000 jars of Cornfield Mickey at $5 per jar. It saved the Chamber of Commerce from going bankrupt and it financially stabilized the little town of Sheffield.

In addition to the big idea of Mickey in the Cornfield, the whole Disney company got behind Mickey's 60th, which became an early synergy model for corporate events. The following, "All Facets of The Walt Disney Company Join in Saluting Mickey Mouse's 60th Birthday", describes many of the marketing strategies incorporated:

> Mickey Mouse will officially mark his 60th birthday on November 18, 1988, and the entire Walt Disney Company is devoting its synergies to observing the milestone throughout the year with special celebrations and events.
>
> The hero himself, Mickey Mouse, joined his fellow screen stars on April 11 to honor their peers at the Academy Awards. New animation and live action brought together Mickey and Tom Selleck on national television for a co-presentation of the Best Animated Short award.
>
> Walt Disney Home Video will release a special Commemorative Edition Mickey Mouse videocassette on May 31. Available for a limited time only, it is a complete and newly created story about Mickey, featuring original animated scenes from some of Mickey's greatest film roles, including the masterpiece "Sorcerer's Apprentice" from the animated classic *Fantasia*.
>
> From May through August, *Earforce One*, a special hot air balloon in the shape of Mickey Mouse's head and wearing a birthday hat, will tour many cities throughout the United States. Traveling with the twelve-story-tall balloon will be the birthday mouse himself who will make personal appearances in each of the cities.
>
> At the Disney theme parks—Disneyland in California and Walt Disney World in Florida—Mickey's 60th birthday will be celebrated with parades, shows, and other sensational offerings throughout the summer months. Walt Disney World has created a new feature, Mickey's Birthdayland, which will be unveiled in June and entertain Magic Kingdom visitors throughout the year.
>
> The Disney Channel is planning specials and retrospective material to air from April to November. Additionally, the *Disney Channel Magazine* will devote articles and activities to Mickey, and will also run a calendar of company-wide birthday events for 1988. Plans are

being made to originate portions of a new Disney Channel television series this fall from Mickey's Birthdayland at Walt Disney World. The daily series will choose some of its audience at Birthdayland to attend shows during production on soundstages at the new Disney-MGM Studios near EPCOT Center.

The Consumer Products Division brings Mickey's birthday to the public with a complete line of new Mickey's 60th merchandise this fall. Special items include a reproduction of the original Ingersoll Mickey Mouse watch and collectible cards free with the purchase of Mickey's 60th merchandise. The merchandise includes a variety of children's books, including a $19.99 facsimile of a 1934 storybook from Abrams and a $250 deluxe book from Another Rainbow. Additionally, Mickey's birthday will be supported by more than 30 major retail chains that will promote retail sales in all product categories.

Walt Disney Pictures is honoring its special star with a new animated logo to replace the Castle logo for 1988. This new piece of animation is a retrospective of Mickey from 1928 to the present. The 60th logo will also appear with many of the Disney film products including selected Disney television shows and home video titles.

Touring the country beginning in August will be Mickey's Diamond Jubilee Ice Show, a fun-filled tribute to the famous mouse starring a host of Disney characters and talented skaters.

A gala television special saluting Mickey's 60th birthday will air on NBC-TV in November. Joining in this hour-long look at Mickey's six decades of merry-making will be many of his longtime character friends and a host of celebrities.

During the year, a gigantic tribute to Mickey Mouse will be visible to commercial airline passengers as they fly across Iowa. Over five million corn plants surrounded by 300 acres of oats have been planted in a field in Sheffield, Iowa, to form Mickey's head. The image of his profile measures 1.1 miles from the tip of his nose to the end of his ear. The unusual "birthday card" will become recognizable to airborne viewers by early summer.

Besides the many domestic company activities, all the international divisions are joining in celebrating Mickey's anniversary. There will be sweepstakes awarding trips to Disneyland and Walt Disney World, special merchandise is being created for international markets, and all Disney international television programming will contain special features surrounding the birthday festivities.

This milestone year is a very special one for Mickey, one that has already generated a great deal of excitement and anticipation. Little did anyone realize sixty years ago, when Mickey Mouse made his debut, the tremendous impact this friendly little personality would have on generations around the world.

CHAPTER TWELVE

Mickey 60th Marches On

There was an abundance of other marketing-based goings-on for Mickey's 60th. I was sent out on a Mickey's 60th tour with Mickey Mouse and two of the original Mouseketeers, Bobby Burgess and Sherry Alberoni. The two-some touted all that was happening at the theme parks and why everyone everywhere should visit Disneyland and Walt Disney World during the birthday celebration. We traveled across the country to many Disney target market cities: Philadelphia, Boston, Detroit, Kansas City, Denver, Salt Lake City, and of course, New York City. In each city it was morning until night interviews, one right after the other, with local print, radio, and TV.

Our New York City adventure was particularly exciting with a multi-day schedule and a host of special events, all of which alerted the media to the Mickey's 60th goings-on. The first saw Mickey and the Mouseketeers making a "surprise" visit to the trading floor of the New York Stock Exchange, then later that same day Mickey, joined by Minnie, visited children at Lenox Hill Hospital. That evening, New York's then Pan Am building (now the MetLife building), a 58-story skyscraper that sits above New York's Grand Central Station in midtown Manhattan, was illuminated with a silhouette of Mickey's face. The image covered floors 36–46 and was visible to onlookers for several miles.

Continuing on day two, New York's Mayor Ed Koch greeted Mickey, Minnie, and the Mouseketeers at the city's South Street Seaport where everyone boarded the historical *DeWitt Clinton* steamboat (to commemorate Mickey's debut in *Steamboat Willie*). Onboard, a ceremony was held at which time Mickey presented Mayor Koch with the key to the new Mickey's Birthdayland at Walt Disney World. They then sounded the *Steamboat Willie* whistle that cued the release of four thousand balloons, live music, and a 35-member drill team that went through their paces.

The steamboat, with special guests and numerous media onboard, became a party boat. *People* magazine hosted the special celebration as we sailed around New York harbor and to the Statue of Liberty. The resulting press coverage included ABC network news, WABC-TV, WNBC-TV, WNYW-TV, WPIX-TV, WOR-TV, WINS Radio, WHTZ-FM, WMCA-AM, *New York Daily News*, *The New York Times*, *New York Post*, *New York Newsday*, *People*, Associated Press, *Adweek*, Gannett Syndicate Gamma-Liaison international photo agency, American Image News, *World Journal*, *Korea Times*, and Birnbaum Travel Guides. In addition, Disney Broadcast Services shot in-house stories on every NYC event and fed them via satellite to thousands of TV stations around the country.

Even more Mickey's 60th special events happened around New York City while we were there. As part of a separate national tour, *Earforce One*, the twelve-and-one-half-story-high hot-air balloon in the shape of Mickey's head that had been created for the 60th celebration was tethered in the city's Battery Park and in Flushing Meadows, the site of the 1964–65 New York World's Fair. Of course the hot air balloon pilots were on hand for media interviews. The balloon itself was quite something to see, as described in this excerpt from a PR piece entitled "Brand New 'Earforce One' Balloon Tours North America in Celebration of Mickey Mouse's 60th Birthday":

> An all-new *Earforce One* hot air balloon, shaped like Mickey Mouse with a birthday hat perched atop his head, will tour North America this spring and summer as part of worldwide festivities honoring the 60th anniversary of Mickey's screen debut in *Steamboat Willie*.

> The tour will commemorate not only Mickey's birthday, but the special birthday celebrations being planned both at Disneyland in California and Walt Disney World in Florida.

> At 125 feet in height, the new hot-air balloon is 25 percent taller than the original 10-story *Earforce One*, the Walt Disney Company's first hot-air balloon, which made its debut in autumn of 1986. Most of the added height is in the colorful birthday hat, 44 feet high and constructed from 42 pieces of fabric.

> The tour will begin May 16 in Vancouver, Canada, traveling to Alaska next and then southward through the Pacific Northwest, California, and Mexico to arrive back at Disneyland in time for a June 3 preview of the park's birthday celebration. The balloon will then proceed eastward through the Southwest and Midwest to arrive in Boston on July 3.

> Thereafter, *Earforce One* will visit other cities in the East, the Midwest, and the South before finishing its tour at Walt Disney World in late August. Each visit will include morning and evening balloon flights and/or tethers. In addition, *Earforce One* will appear at major league baseball games along the route whenever it is convenient to do so.

> Manufactured by Cameron Balloons, Ltd., of Bristol, England, the balloon is over 12 stories tall. Each of Mickey's ears is 34 feet in

diameter, his nose is 33 feet long, and his eye alone is 16 feet high. The balloon was constructed from 23,668 square feet of fabric and weighs (uninflated and minus the basket) 363 pounds.

In addition to celebrating his birthday in New York, the icon of the Disney Company and Roy E. Disney took a very special, first-time Disney trip to Russia that year. As was described in an article by Disney historian Jim Korkis, the duo were officially invited to attend the first Soviet-sponsored Disney Animation Festival. Roy Disney explained, "The festival came about because the Soviets had come to Disney and asked if the company would be interested in bringing some of our films over there. They said, "It's the beginning of a new era. It's much bigger than just Disney and Mickey Mouse coming to the Soviet Union. It's two countries coming closer together and it's very exciting. Everyone loves Mickey here.'"

On behalf of the company, Roy accepted the invitation.

The Disney Animation Festival was sponsored by the Soviet Commission on Cinematography and was kicked off with a gala premiere in Moscow. It was the first time Disney films, except for *Snow White and the Seven Dwarfs*, had officially and legally been viewed in the U.S.S.R. Tickets were sold out weeks in advance, but Disney insisted that children from local orphanages be invited for free to the screenings in Moscow, Leningrad, and Tallinn. In addition to classic shorts featuring Mickey and Donald Duck, audiences had the opportunity to legally see *Snow White and the Seven Dwarfs, Bambi, One Hundred and One Dalmatians*, and *Fantasia*.

Soviet audiences were familiar with the Disney characters, but dialog in English was still a challenge. So, Soviet actors were hired to simultaneously read translated scripts during the screening after being coached on the characters and the voice inflections.

A costumed Mickey Mouse joined a costumed Misha the Bear, the mascot for the 1980 Moscow Olympics, for a tour of Red Square. Interesting, the Russian children kept a discreet distance from Mickey and just politely waved. However, they swarmed around Misha with much laughter. Maybe it was because Mickey was so uncharacteristically tall, probably in the 5'8" or 5'9" range. The Mouse usually stands about 5' or so.

Tony Perri, a Disneyland broadcast producer who accompanied Roy Disney and Mickey Mouse on the Russian tour to document the trip explained why the character wasn't the most perfect for the task: "Interestingly, because the company didn't want to spend the money to take Mickey Mouse from Disneyland or Walt Disney World, we picked up a costumed Mickey character from the Disney offices in Frankfort, Germany. In doing so, we ended up with a strangely tall mouse."

Also during the trip, Roy E. Disney and other Disney executives visited the famed Russian animation studio, Soyuzmultfilm Studios. Roy said.

"Though some of their technology was primitive, their creativity makes up for it and their work is really good."

While there, a special cartoon was presented to Roy, titled *The Marathon*. "It was an absolutely beautiful tribute to Mickey. We were all choked up. My wife was in tears."

A little over two minutes in length, the cartoon shows a young boy in black silhouette going to a line that divides the screen image in half. It is like a mirror with the young boy on one side and the classic black-and-white Mickey Mouse in black silhouette on the other side. At the top of the screen is the number 1928, the year Mickey debuted. The number clicks to a zero and starts clicking upwards to the number 60. During this time, in silhouette the young boy ages through the stages of growing up, from a young man and finally to an old man.

During the short, Mickey and the other character have fun dancing and playing until the ravages of age slows down the old man. Mickey whistles to call over a chair for the man to sit on. Another young boy runs up to the man and is directed back to the line where the number clicks back to zero and the assumption is that the same adventure will be repeated again with this new boy and an ageless Mickey.

The director Misha Tumelya and animators Sasha Dorogov and Alexandr Petrov presented this short to Roy as a tribute for the 60th anniversary of Mickey. Roy recalled:

"Really, quite literally, we all wound up hugging each other with tears coming down our faces...it was one of the more emotional moments that I can remember in my life."

Tony Perri, meantime, was putting together a series of video packages covering the trip for satellite feed to TV stations all over the world. He said, "I remember we stayed at the Ukraina Hotel and we edited the pieces in my room. We put together several international news packages and worked with Russian facilities to be able to feed the videos out via satellite. Everybody from *Entertainment Tonight* to every U.S. television network and television stations all over the world picked up the stories. The whole concept was a huge marketing win."

CHAPTER THIRTEEN

The Late Eighties and Beyond

We could always count on big Disney events being covered by the media masses. However, there were times when small happenings also resulted in enormous press coverage. Such was the case in 1988 during Mickey's 60th when Mickey Moo, a Holstein cow with a large natural marking of Mickey Mouse's head on its side, joined the Disneyland cast. And how did a cow with a Mickey marking find its way to Anaheim?

The story goes that the Midwest farmer and owner of the unique animal sent a photo of it bearing the unmistakable image of Mickey Mouse's head on its side (black Mickey image against a mostly white cow) to the Disney company. Somehow, Michael Eisner got wind of it, saw the image, and decided to purchase the cow, name it, and put it on display for guests at Big Thunder Ranch in Frontierland at Disneyland. Named Mickey Moo, the cow made its debut to media in a song-and-dance introductory event devised by the Disneyland Entertainment Division and held at the corral at the Big Thunder Ranch.

A large theatrical curtain served as a backdrop for a line of dancers attired in farmer garb that came bopping onto the scene to the music of "A Cow Named Caroline" from the hit musical *Gypsy*, except that a Disney parody of that number was written for the newly named Mickey Moo. The revised lyrics included the opening stanza, "I have a moo cow, a new cow, a true cow, named...Mickey Moo". At the end of the number came the big buildup to the curtain opening to reveal Disneyland's newest cast member.

We had a moderate local press turnout, so media coverage was thought to be iffy at best. Some doubted that we would get any press pick-up at all, including Scott Brinegar, a freelance photographer who worked with us on the publicity team, and Renie Bardeau, Disneyland's long-time chief photographer. They had checked out the cow prior to the "reveal" presentation. Brinegar recalled, "Renie and I went backstage to the pony farm to look at the cow before the media event. I recall we both said, 'Nobody is going to care about this cow with the shape of Mickey Mouse's head on its side. It's silly!'"

But they dutifully took photos of the bovine that the Publicity Department distributed to the national news media while the Disneyland broadcast group put together a story package of the Mickey Moo press event that was fed, via satellite, to news stations across the country.

As it turned out, we were all were dead wrong about the media interest level in Mickey Moo. The coverage was massive. Not only did photos of Mickey Moo appear in print in every nook and cranny throughout the United States, but Mickey Moo became a worldwide bovine star. Television news reported the story as did radio stations everywhere. It was incredible! Ultimately, Mickey Moo lived a happy and leisurely life at Disneyland, having thousands, if not millions, of photos of her taken by guests until her passing in the 1990s.

After that surprise success story, Disneyland was deluged with photos from people all over the world who claimed to own animals with Mickey Mouse markings. Pictures of dogs, cats, horses, birds, hamsters, and every variety of animal species came pouring in. Someone even sent in a photo of a potato that was shaped like Mickey. However, no images ever lived up to the natural Mickey likeness sported by Mickey Moo. She was indeed the most photographed cow in history.

One of my favorite press events during 1988 that I was lucky enough to attend as a guest rather than a working publicist was the opening of Disney's Grand Floridian Hotel and Spa, a luxury resort at Walt Disney World in Orlando. Hundreds of media were invited to attend what was one of the most elegant openings ever to take place on Disney World property. In keeping with the property's architectural theme that was inspired by Victorian-era beach resorts, the hotel is reminiscent of the famous Hotel Del Coronado in San Diego, California. It is stunning. But what made this opening so amazing to me was how far the Walt Disney World Marketing and Entertainment staff went to create the opulence of the era.

The opening event was held inside the hotel's massive five-story lobby, a space that features a stunning stained glass dome, Italian marble floors with inlays of various Disney characters, and infused with a sophisticated and welcoming Victorian ambiance. A full orchestra in formal attire played on the hotel's second balcony overlooking the lobby and the special guests, Florida's governor along with Burt Reynolds and Loni Anderson (who were the hot celebrity couple of the day), arrived on the property by helicopter.

But here's my favorite part—Walt Disney World staff had rented nearly every black tuxedo from Atlanta to Orlando to outfit each male press attendee in the appropriate dress for what was a very elegant Victorian affair. Women were provided with evening gloves. The men were each measured for a tuxedo upon hotel check-in and their perfectly cleaned, pressed, and fitted suits were delivered to their rooms on the day of the opening party. Talk about going the extra mile!

Phil Lengyel, then senior vice president of Walt Disney World Marketing, remembered the tuxedo rentals: "We never considered doing those kind of things an extravagance. We considered it a necessary "aha" to get the media's attention and have them talking about us in ways that they otherwise might not. You have to put them in tuxedos, you've got to have Burt Reynolds there. This is an elegant, upscale hotel. Being formally dressed was what people wore in the Victorian time period that the resort represented."

Less than a year later, the Florida marketing group was preparing its campaign for the opening of a new theme park, Disney-MGM Studios. Lengyel recalled that Marketing needed something to promote the new park in their target cities (geographic locations that fed park attendance in high numbers and where marketing dollars were often spent locally on advertising, promotions, and publicity) throughout the United States: "At the time, we'd go in and blitz a market for a very intense period of time. Frank Wells liked to call our target market teams hit squads. For example, we'd go into Boston and we would partner with a radio station and we'd stage a contest to say, 'Win trips to Walt Disney World!'. But then we took that a step further. We'd work with the city administration and plan a civic-hosted Disney parade in the city to kick off a host of activities."

The Walt Disney World marketing group would then work with a retailer; so, for instance, in Boston it might be Filene's Department Store to host elements of Disney World in store. Lengyel explained, "We'd create a Walt Disney World area in their housewares department and bring in Disney chefs. In another corner of the store we'd bring in our horticulture staff. We brought all these little pieces, parts of Walt Disney World, into the town and activated them around the city where people could kind of experience it and see what a Walt Disney World vacation might be like. Hopefully, it would entice them to book a trip as a result of those experiences."

The taste of Disney World was replicated in New York, Boston, Chicago, Philadelphia, Detroit, Atlanta, Miami...every place where the Orlando resort had a large footprint in terms of attendance importance. "We just kind of picked up the resort and brought it to that city," said Lengyel.

Thinking about putting together a target market blitz for the opening of the Disney-MGM Studios, Lengyel explained, "We wanted to put together a promotion that was reminiscent of a Hollywoodesque studio. We went to California and found a guy who did customized limousines and we told him that we wanted a tricked-out car that we would call the LiMouseine. The car had to be the most elaborate, luxurious, and unbelievable vehicle ever."

The LiMouseine, of course, was to be the personal vehicle of the big cheese himself, Mickey Mouse, who would arrive in Walt Disney World's target markets across the country in style. Lengyel said, "Because we needed it to be extra-special for promotional purposes, we decided that we needed to have a working radio booth in the car so that when Mickey traveled from city to city, DJs could be picked up along the way and they could broadcast their shows live from the vehicle."

Mickey Mouse rode in high style on a 37-city tour promoting the opening of the Disney-MGM Studios in the forty-foot-long LiMouseine. Some of the car's special features included four cellular phones (a big deal since mobile phones were a rare commodity at that time), a radio remote DJ booth, two Sony TVs with VCRs (this was well before DVDs arrived on the scene), and four sunroofs. But the crowning glory was the hood ornament—a 24-carat, gold-plated Tinker Bell.

On May 1, 1989, the Disney-MGM Studios (renamed Disney's Hollywood Studios in 2008), opened with much fanfare. The opening day dedication of the park read: "The world you have entered was created by The Walt Disney Company and is dedicated to Hollywood—not a place on a map, but a state of mind that exists wherever people dream and wonder and imagine, a place where illusion and reality are fused by technological magic. We welcome you to a Hollywood that never was—and always will be."

Despite the intermittent rain that day, the Disney-MGM Studios was packed. It was the largest opening day press event in Walt Disney World history up until that time. The park was so crowded that officials had to close its parking lot at only 9:15 a.m., just about an hour after opening.

Among the Hollywood legends who were on hand and who helped Michael Eisner cut the filmstrip ribbon dedicating the park were George Burns and Bob Hope. Countless press stories flooded worldwide media, in print, on radio, and via TV, many of which were fed via satellite to home stations. The launch of the new park was a huge success.

Other ongoing small, but still important, marketing opportunities included producing PSAs (Public Service Announcements) using the theme parks as a backdrop. Such pieces focused on such topics as emergency preparedness or featured Smokey the Bear educating the public about the danger of forest fires. PSAs are usually 30 seconds in length and placed on TV stations and radio media at no cost. The objective of the spots is raising awareness and/or changing public attitudes and behavior toward a social issue. Of course for Disney, the objective was also getting free air-time and showcasing the characters and the parks.

Disneyland's Tony Perri produced a number of Disney PSAs. One that he recalled starred Snow White and the Seven Dwarfs shining the spotlight on daylight saving time: "We staged a little bedroom for Snow White in the Clock Shop on Main Street. We show her asleep, with a clock on a bedside table as the Seven Dwarfs sneak in and turn her clock ahead one hour. The final voiceover says, "Don't forget to move your clock ahead one hour for daylight saving time. And do it for someone you love."

"Remember to Vote" was another one. Perri said, "We used the Seven Dwarfs again for this one. What we did was have all of them piling into an old-fashioned voting booth that we set up on Main Street and tipping it over. The closing shot was Dopey sticking his head out of the fray with the voice-over saying, "Remember to vote on November 4th, but do it one at a time."

With theme park marketing on the fast track for large and small projects alike, 1989 ushered in the opening of a new attraction in Bear Country at Disneyland, called Splash Mountain. It was the first "E" ticket ride to open under the auspices of Eisner and Wells' revitalization of the park. The new log flume attraction opened on Disneyland's 34th birthday, July 17, 1989. According to the Disneyland press release on the attraction:

> Splash Mountain takes guests on a waterborne journey via a buoyant log through the backwoods, swamps, and bayous of the Old South as it was depicted in the Disney movie *Song of the South*. Showcased in 15 scenes from the motion picture, whimsical music and the mischievous antics of 103 Audio-Animatronics figures provide a rich audio-visual treat for guests as they experience thrilling lifts and drops in a fast water ride.

The attraction contained three water drops, two small and one ride-ending thriller. At the top of the final hill, the ride vehicle descends a 52-foot drop at a 45-degree angle, reaching a maximum speed of 40 mph. As it goes over the precipice of the hill, a stationary camera snaps images of riders, usually screaming, at exactly the right moment. The images, framed in a Splash Mountain presentation folder, are then made available for sale to those who wish to commemorate the moment.

Splash Mountain was one of the first new attraction ideas presented several years earlier to the then newly installed Eisner and Wells team. While they both loved the concept, Eisner was eager to include a synergy component. The name for the attraction at that time was "Zip-A-Dee-Doo-Dah River Run", a moniker Eisner did not like. He suggested that the Imagineers add a mermaid to the attraction so they could tie it into the recent Disney hit film *Splash* that had starred Daryl Hannah and Tom Hanks. The Imagineers convinced Eisner that this wasn't a good idea, but he was still insistent that the attraction's name be changed. He just didn't think "Zip-A-Dee River Run" would appeal to the teenage audience, the target group for this ride.

When someone suggested they add the word "mountain" after the word "splash," making the attraction title Splash Mountain, everyone knew they had hit upon the perfect name, as this would add a new peak to the Disneyland skyline that already included the Matterhorn, Space Mountain, and Big Thunder Mountain. And while the name ultimately didn't directly connect to the film *Splash*, having that word in the title surely didn't hurt.

Disneyland's 35th anniversary kicked off in January 1990 with all the marketing bells and whistles that highlighted such year-long celebrations. One of the more special events staged during the year involved bringing back the original hosts of the TV special that opened Disneyland in 1955. Art Linkletter and Bob Cummings were on hand, as was a very special guest, President Ronald Reagan, once again in the Disney spotlight. This time, however, it was immediately post-presidency, but no less exciting to have the former president back at Disneyland.

Reagan's involvement (his first big public event after leaving the White House) included appearing in the finale of the park's celebratory "Party Gras" parade. Riding in a vintage firetruck, with Michael Eisner in the front seat with the driver, Reagan stood in back waving to the cheering crowd as it made its way down Main Street, U.S.A. Media wielding cameras were everywhere, including a host of Disneyland photographers shooting Reagan from every angle. Oops, I shouldn't put it that way. As I was advised from photographer Scott Brinegar who was there, "You don't 'shoot' the president, you photograph him."

Following the parade, Reagan participated in a 35th anniversary salute that took place on a stage on the upper platform of the Main Street Train Station in Town Square. Featuring Ronald Reagan, Michael Eisner, Frank Wells, Roy Disney, Art Linkletter, and Bob Cummings, the commemorative ceremony ended with daytime fireworks and a blast of confetti shot from confetti cannons. The sound of the blast reverberated with a big "bang". At that moment, Reagan instinctively flinched, turned to Michael Eisner, and said, "Missed me."

CHAPTER FOURTEEN

Muppetland

It was 1990 when The Walt Disney Company first became interested in acquiring the Muppets. The possibility of bringing Kermit, Miss Piggy, and friends into the Disney fold held infinite marketing possibilities. Of course, the Muppet opportunity immediately inspired a big idea from Disney creative mastermind Jack Lindquist. It was a radical concept that would turn Disneyland, as we know it, upside-down. Lindquist explained, "When it was announced that the Muppets were going to join the Disney family, I came up with an idea for a year-long promotion that would change Disneyland into Muppetland."

In doing so, he also devised a complete storyline behind the concept. "Mickey and Minnie would welcome Kermit and all the Muppets to Disneyland in a media event, of course. During the welcome, Kermit would surprisingly say to Mickey, 'You know, you've been here a long time. Why don't you, Minnie, Donald, Pluto, and Goofy go on a vacation and we'll look after Disneyland for you.'"

The idea would then be to send the ousted Disney troupe on a world tour to every corner of the globe where they would be welcomed to each city with media coverage. In the meantime, the minute the Disney group departed Disneyland (with much media hoopla), Miss Piggy would convince Kermit that the Muppets are bigger than any mice or ducks and they needed to transform Disneyland into their own place, calling it "Muppetland".

"We planned to change the enormous Disneyland marquee that read "Disneyland" by crossing out the "Disney" part of the word and replacing it with "Muppet" so it would then read 'Muppetland'", Lindquist said. "We were also going to put a gigantic inflatable Kermit atop the sign. At the Disneyland Main Gate, the instantly recognizable flower Mickey planter would be changed to having Kermit, Miss Piggy, and some of the other Muppets enshrined in blossoms. All Disneyland merchandise would disappear in the park with only Muppet character products stocked in the park venues."

The topper was when Lindquist suggested to the horror of many that, "We paint the Matterhorn green, all 147 feet of it."

As always, Lindquist's reasoning contained a clever marketing hook. "Every day hundreds of thousands of people driving the 5 Freeway (from which Space Mountain can be viewed) will see the green mountain. That will get everyone talking."

The entire Muppet promotion was to last for one year, kicking off on January 1, 1991, before everything turned back to normal. Needless to say, there were many, many Disneyland marketing staffers who thought the idea was tantamount to sacrilege. Lindquist recalled, "After a year of traveling around the world, Mickey will have gotten wind of the Muppets takeover of his home, sending him and the gang right back to Anaheim to straighten things out. They get back to Disneyland quite unexpectedly (expectedly prompting another media event). Mickey explains how he trusted his Muppet friends to take care of Disneyland, not take it over. But Miss Piggy, who always had her eye on Mickey anyway, wins him over as apologies abound."

Rather than banish the Muppets from his home turf, Mickey, good Mouse that he is, announces that a new land called "Toontown" is going to be built at Disneyland where the Muppets will be welcome to live forever. A happy ending for all. The Muppet deal was practically signed, sealed, and delivered until the truly unexpected happened.

As blogger Jim Hill reported in *The Huffington Post*:

> Everyone from Michael Eisner on down just loved Jack Lindquist's idea. Especially Jim Henson, who, as it turns out, was a huge Disneyland fan. So as 1990 got underway, plans for this year-long marketing event to happen in 1991 began to filter out through the various divisions at Disney. Scripts were written. Sample ads were created. Models of parade floats were built. And then—on May 16, 1990—Jim Henson died suddenly from an untreated bacterial infection.
>
> At this point, The Walt Disney Company's attempt to acquire the Muppets began to go off-track. With Jim gone, the Henson family had serious second thoughts.

As the months wore on with no signed deal, Lindquist reluctantly tabled the Muppets-take-over-Disneyland idea. Upon giving the whole concept a second think-through about Mickey, Minnie, Donald, Pluto, and Goofy leaving the park, even for a limited period of time, Eisner said to Lindquist, "We probably shouldn't mess around with the family jewels anyway." Lindquist recalled wistfully, "He was right, but it would have been fun."

However, it wasn't quite the end for the Muppets and Disney at that time. After about six months of legal wrangling, the two companies came to a limited agreement per the use of the Henson characters.

Disney was granted an 18-month license to enable them to present *Jim Henson's MuppetVision 3D*, a film that the company had been working on with

Henson prior to his death. The movie starring the Henson crew debuted at Disney-MGM Studios in May 1991. Thirteen years later, in February 2004, The Walt Disney Company finally did sign a contract with the Jim Henson Company to acquire the Muppets and the Bear in the Big Blue House.

Better late than never, but Kermit and Miss Piggy's Muppetland was never to be.

CHAPTER FIFTEEN

Elizabeth Taylor and Lavender Fireworks

Capturing PR for Disneyland came in many different packages. Sometimes it was generated for a new attraction opening such as Splash Mountain, sometimes to celebrate an anniversary, and sometimes to welcome special guests. Many celebrities have visited Disneyland over the years; its official guest book reads like a Who's Who of 20th (and early 21st) century pop culture.

With its proximity to Hollywood and the celebrity haven of Los Angeles, Disneyland has always been a place for celebrities to enjoy themselves with their friends and families, as well as, on occasion, a place to garner some fun publicity exposure with a photo on their favorite attraction or with their favorite Disney character.

One Hollywood legend truly took Disneyland to heart. On February 27, 1992, Elizabeth Taylor and her then husband, Larry Fortensky, bought the park for an evening to celebrate her 60th birthday.

The night was filled with celebrities, as Taylor invited one thousand of her closest friends to the private event. The *Los Angeles Times* reported on the extravaganza:

> Elizabeth Taylor swooped into Disneyland in a horse-drawn white carriage Thursday night as hundreds of her Hollywood friends turned out to salute a "survivor" on her 60th birthday. The woman who grew up on screen before the rapt eyes of generations of Americans transformed Disneyland's Fantasyland into a movie extravaganza with hundreds of celebrities, extraordinary security, and lights that turned night into day.
>
> Trumpet fanfares and flashing strobe lights greeted the celebrities who preceded her to Sleeping Beauty Castle. Disney characters escorted everyone from Henry Winkler to Cheryl Tiegs, Gregory Peck to Tom Selleck. A blonde Delta Burke, accompanied by her husband, Gerald McRaney, called Taylor "strong and soft...witty and clever, intelligent...a fighter".

Disneyland officials barred the press from the event, but beamed their own videotape of the festivities onto satellite for waiting television stations. It gave the public another glimpse of the woman who starred in *National Velvet* at age 12, won two Oscars, and married seven men, one of them twice. Along the way she battled a host of illnesses and addictions to painkillers.

"This is a private party and the sky is the limit," said a Disney spokeswoman. No one would say how much it cost to fête the hundreds of invited guests, but the normal $8,000 charge to rent the park after hours clearly was only the starting point. Although corporations have staged parties at Disneyland in the past, Taylor was the first individual to rent it, a park spokesman said.

Songwriter Carol Bayer Sager, one of the party organizers, said she "wanted to just throw a party where Elizabeth could have fun. She has brought a lot of love into my life." Her longtime friend Roddy McDowall beamed as he arrived and said, "It's wonderful to be here to celebrate a survivor."

Jon Voight, wearing a white Lakers jacket, said: "I remember her when *National Velvet* came out and I fell in love with her. She means so much to us."

Rod McKuen said he wrote a song as his gift to Taylor, but wouldn't say more because it's "a very private thing". Actor John Forsythe said the gift from him and his wife was a donation to the American Foundation for AIDS Research, the charity for which Taylor has raised money.

Shirley MacLaine, who arrived with journalist Carl Bernstein, said Taylor has been "the most long-lasting star on the firmament and I know about that cosmic stuff...I'm here in celebration of what has been a fantasy life". *Times* columnist Liz Smith, who attended the party, gave this report as events began to unfold:

"Disneyland was just spectacular. Sleeping Beauty Castle was decorated with columns of lavender and gold balloons. Vintage cars carried the guests. Trumpets sounded as each alighted. Security was rigid, but the atmosphere was warm, informal, and childlike. Elizabeth Taylor and Larry Fortensky arrived at 9:30 pm. She was wearing sparkling cowboy boots and black quilted jacket with sprays of sequins, and he was wearing a black leather jacket and brown cowboy boots. Mickey Mouse took her arm as she got out of her limo and walked with her."

The extravaganza was a remarkable tribute to a woman who has not made a featured motion picture since 1980, nor a television movie since 1989. In recent years she has been known for her perfumes, her work on behalf of people with AIDS, and her latest marriage, last October, to construction worker Larry Fortensky, 20 years her junior.

Park officials shooed the public out at 6 pm and imposed extraordinary security inside and outside the grounds. Disneyland cast members sported wristbands in addition to their regular identification badges to cut down on the chance of infiltrators. Outside the park, guards with flashlights and German shepherd dogs were stationed at intervals of 50 feet.

Mark French, 23, a tourist from Nowra, Australia, said he was rushed by Disney officials who were counting down the minutes at the end of the day: "I was trying to get a picture with Mickey and they told me I had to leave. I knew Liz Taylor was going to be here, so I thought about hiding someplace so I could see her."

The Federal Aviation Administration restricted airspace over the park until midnight, letting news media helicopters swing over the park two at a time. Taylor said before the party that she invited "everyone I know and like and respect" for a "wild and fun" evening to contrast with her marriage ceremony to Fortensky, whom she met in a drug rehabilitation clinic. Those nuptials, at the Neverland ranch of entertainer Michael Jackson, near Santa Barbara, were "very small and controlled", Taylor said.

Lindsay Schnebly, a Disneyland broadcast producer at the time, interviewed Taylor and Fortensky upon their arrival, and recalled, "I remember standing in front of the flower Mickey at the entrance to the park. We had a little stage built and had set up lights to do the interview. She and Fortensky, who was wearing a cowboy hat, arrived as the Goodyear blimp was flying overhead with the flashing message "Happy Birthday, Elizabeth" along its side."

For whatever reason, Michael Eisner walked up to Schnebly with the pair for the interview.

As Schnebly began the Q&A with Taylor, who he described as "looking like a million bucks", Fortensky removed his cowboy hat and handed it to Eisner. Schnebly said, "I'm interviewing them both and there stands Michael Eisner trying to not look like 'I don't know why I'm holding this hat'."

When Schnebly completed his questioning of Taylor, he ended the interview by asking her, "Is there anything that I haven't asked you that you'd like to add?" According to Schnebly, "She got a very sexy look in her eyes and emphatically said, 'You've just got to go out and take life by the horns and enjoy it!' There was a suitable pause and Eisner looks at us and says, 'Sounds good to me!'"

The Taylor, Fortensky, Eisner interview was incorporated into the story package video fed via satellite to TV stations all over the world. Since Disneyland Broadcast Services was the only crew allowed to cover the private birthday party inside the park that night, press clamored for the footage.

Taylor's final interview response of "Taking life by the horns and enjoying it" and Eisner's "Sounds good to me" response turned out to be the most used clip in the entire story. In fact, the entire packaged story was the single most used video news report of the year.

Highlights of the event included each celebrity guest boarding a vintage automobile decorated with orchids in front of the Main Street Train Station and being driven down the avenue to the forecourt of Sleeping Beauty Castle where Barry Manilow kicked off the festivities singing "I Made it Through the Rain".

Taylor and Fortensky were transported to the location in a white horse-drawn carriage. Guests then walked through Sleeping Beauty Castle into the Fantasyland party location while trumpeters, folk dancers, jugglers, bands, and Mickey and his friends entertained guests. An extravagant lavender (Taylor's favorite color) fireworks display was also incorporated into the evening's celebration. Taylor remarked at the end of it all: "This was the best party of my life."

Hollywood and the Disney parks had previously come together within a more conventional Hollywood setting—a movie premiere. Celebs were a key ingredient for a high-profile movie premiere that partnered The Walt Disney Studios in California with Walt Disney World in Florida.

It was spring 1990 and the studio was getting ready to release the film *Dick Tracy*, starring Warren Beatty (who also produced and directed) and Madonna, with Al Pacino, Charles Durning, and Dustin Hoffman in supporting roles. Walt Disney World was getting ready to open what was then an unbelievable multi-screen movie theater, the AMC 10, on Pleasure Island, a youth-oriented entertainment and dining district on the property.

Phil Lengyel, the senior vice president of Walt Disney World Resort Marketing, recalled, "We needed to add sizzle to our movie theater opening. We worked with Jeffrey Katzenberg and Dick Cook who was then president of Buena Vista Pictures Distribution, to hold the world premiere of the Touchstone film at our new movie complex in June of that year. Of course, we couldn't just leave it at that. We wanted to have the stars of the film over to the Disney-MGM Studios as well because we were promoting that venue, too."

The plan was to invite thousands of press from all over the world to the movie premiere as part of a four-day media event that would also include promotionally showcasing other Walt Disney World venues and attractions. Michael Eisner was scheduled to hold an important press conference during the festivities to announce new projects as part of what was then called "The Disney Decade".

With regard to the *Dick Tracy* premiere, Disney World marketing execs decided to add an "aha" factor to their plans. To get all invited media and celebrity guests into the Tracy mood, they provided everyone with a yellow fedora (like Dick Tracy wore in the film). Thousands of hats were purchased and waiting in guests' hotel rooms upon check-in. "And, by God, they wore them!" said Lengyel.

The film debut was held on the evening of June 14, 1990, at the AMC 10 on Pleasure Island. Warren Beatty led a procession of celebrities down a red carpet into theater number five. The theater was filled to capacity with Hollywood stars, media, local dignitaries, and special guests...most wearing yellow fedoras.

Following the premiere, everyone was escorted to the Disney-MGM Studios where an extravagant party was held. As the *Los Angeles Times* reported:

> Disney throws parties the way Tolstoy wrote novels. From the bus caravans to the fireworks display, this was a fiesta on the grand scale. Food stations were set up throughout the park with barbecued shrimp, seafood cassoulet, roast beef, lamb chops, fettuccine derby, and for the more daring diners, "snails California".

All the attractions at the park were open, celebs arrived via parade, Hoffman and Beatty were immortalized in cement in the forecourt of the Chinese Theater at the Disney-MGM Studios, and there were two performances of two Tracy-themed musicals.

In fact, the *Dick Tracy* project permeated many divisions of The Walt Disney Company as the synergy wheels turned throughout the organization to support the film. Merchandise was created, television specials were run, books were published, and theme park shows and parades were produced, among many vehicles that showcased the movie.

The one downside of the entire campaign was that the film itself did not receive the accolades that Disney had hoped it would. However, it was ultimately considered a box office and awards success. It picked up seven Academy Award nominations and won in three of the categories: Best Original Song, Best Makeup, and Best Art Direction.

PART TWO

Marketing Inside the Company

CHAPTER SIXTEEN

The "S" Word

My years working at Disneyland in Publicity were so much fun. Of course, it was also a lot of hard work, long hours, and sometimes a seven-day-a-week job. It taught me how to be a team player. And what an education in marketing! I couldn't have learned more if I had gone to Harvard and earned a degree in that discipline.

But after six years inside the Magic Kingdom, I was ready for a move upward and there didn't seem to be any opportunities on the horizon at Disneyland. I seized an opportunity to return to Burbank and the corporate headquarters at The Walt Disney Studios as manager of a new and unique department called Corporate Synergy and Special Projects.

If there was one word that defined what working inside the Disney marketing machine meant during the era of Michael Eisner and Frank Wells, that word was synergy. Defined simply as "working together", synergy is a high-profile business concept that, when strategically incorporated into a diversified company, can elevate high-priority projects to dizzying marketing heights at the consumer level. But, and it's a big but, synergy must start at the very top of a company where it is fostered as an important, indeed vital, marketing tool to make it work.

Of course, the concept of synergy had always been around the Disney organization—since 1929, in fact, when a stranger walked up to Walt Disney in a hotel lobby and offered him $300 to put Mickey Mouse's likeness on a children's pencil tablet. Walt, needing the money, accepted, and in turn, launched the business unit that would one day become Disney Licensing. Walt had opened the door to a valuable new asset for the company, the concept of synergy. Walt's brother and business partner, Roy, initially called this cross-utilization of resources "integration".

The concept of synergy hit its peak in corporate America in the 1980s and '90s, although few organizations took advantage of making it work in their companies, certainly not in any way close to the way Disney did it. Why? I suspect there are two reasons:

- Because the companies did not have a CEO or president that believed synergy could really catch on despite the almost limitless possibilities if it was integrated properly within the company.
- No one had a clue how to make disparate business units, all contained within their own silos and with their own agendas, step into each other's marketing domain and work together harmoniously.

Although a hot concept at the time, synergy was often derided as an empty theory, a buzzword, and a bark without a bite. Michael Eisner once remarked, "The term synergy may be the object of ridicule throughout the world, but not at Disney. This concept of cross-promotion and transformation of popular products into new media is an engine that helps drive our company. Synergy, for us, goes with creativity—which rhymes with selectivity—which means keeping one's eye on the ball."

But even today, using the word synergy is often derided, leading to such 21st century euphemisms as partnership marketing, franchise marketing, and business intelligence, among others. It's still synergy, even if corporations can't bring themselves to use the "s" word.

However, I can assure you, when it came to Disney and incorporating synergy components into its marketing vision for company priorities, it was a powerful word that meant unbelievable success, the extra edge that elevated everything to a higher level. Under Eisner and Wells, The Walt Disney Company became a well-oiled synergy machine where each business unit served as an important cog in the wheel that made the whole work more successfully.

Eisner and Wells were without question the kings of the synergy hill in corporate America in the late 1980s into the '90s. They inspired it, cultivated it, promoted it, worked it, and made it an everyday part of the Disney lexicon. Their thinking was in lockstep with the company's founder, Walt Disney, who, as previously described, may have been the first Hollywood executive to realize synergy's potential. Walt's strategy was illustrated in the following excerpt from a *Wall Street Journal* article from February 4, 1958, entitled "Walt's Profit Formula: Dream, Diversify—and Never Miss An Angle":

> The formula: Wring every possible profitable squeal and squeak out of such assets as the Three Little Pigs and Mickey Mouse—first by diversifying into a wide variety of activities, then by dovetailing them so all work to exploit one another.
>
> Walter E. Disney and his crew of starry-eyed artists and ingenious innovators are by all odds kings of the kid frontier. But they're also shrewd businessmen who inhabit no financial fantasyland. And companies beset by earnings' erosion may find some profit-making pointers by elbowing the kids aside and taking a look at the integrated

doings in the wondrous world of Walt Disney Productions.

"Integration is the key word around here; we don't do anything in one line without giving a thought to its likely profitability in our other lines," says Roy Disney, President of WDP and older brother of Chairman Walt. To see what Roy Disney means, consider *Sleeping Beauty*, a cartoon epic currently in the WDP works. This 70-or-so-minute film, already three years in the making, won't hit theatre screens until Christmas. But the fairy tale already is paying off for Disney.

For example, at Disneyland, the film has been transformed into colorfully animated dioramas complete with trick photography to make them come alive. Children and adults line up, sometimes four abreast, for the 10-minute walk through the Sleeping Beauty attraction at 35 cents a head.

Another Disney department, Licensing, also has gone to work on *Sleeping Beauty*, lining up toy makers, garment producers and others interested in making articles based on *Sleeping Beauty* characters. *Sleeping Beauty* also is getting the build-up treatment on the publishing front, with New York's Simon & Schuster pouring various versions of the fairy tale into the nation's bookstores.

By early October, with the start of the fall television season, *Beauty* will be stirring on the nation's TV sets as Disney script writers work in repeated references to the coming film on such programs as *Disneyland* and, perhaps, put together a special program or two about it. A month later, WDP's phonograph record division will be spewing forth platters based on music from the film. And about six weeks before the movie is released, the studio's comic strip artists will launch the *Sleeping Beauty* story in Disney's own syndicated newspaper cartoon strips.

And *Sleeping Beauty* won't fade away after the movie's showing. The cycle will be run through again in much the same fashion in country after country until nearly every moppet in the free world has had the chance of seeing the movie and buying a doll, reading a book, following a comic strip, and hearing a tune based on *Sleeping Beauty*. Even then there still will be life—and profits—left in *Sleeping Beauty*. Seven years after her screen debut *Sleeping Beauty*, in the form of a re-issued film, again will make the rounds of the world's theaters.

"Walt," says a close associate, "supplies ideas for every phase of this business—ideas for new films, for new features in the park, for new merchandise, even for new songs. But it's his brother Roy who keeps him from getting carried away and makes sure that the company's financial feet are always solidly on the ground."

Accompanying the above 1958 *Wall Street Journal* article was an illustration of how Disney "integration" permeated the company at that time.

Depicted was a central film asset (such as *Sleeping Beauty*) with an out-growth of lines to an array of related company properties that in very precise ways infused value into and in turn supported the central theme. The lines crisscrossed each other going this way and that to every division of the company. Walt Disney's vision in this "map" defined his company's key assets, stemming from a valuable and unique core, and identified patterns of complementary benefits.

Shown within the one-page illustration was a range of entertainment-related assets—books and comic books, music, TV, a magazine, a theme park, merchandise licensing—surrounding a core of theatrical films. It illustrates a dense web of synergistic connections, primarily between the core and other assets. Comic strips promote films; films feed material to comic strips. The theme park, Disneyland, plugs movies, and movies plug the park. TV publicizes products of the music division, and the film division feeds "tunes and talent" to the music division.

The *Journal* article put Walt's theory into words:

> Disney sustains value-creating growth by developing an unrivaled capability in family-friendly animated (and live-action) films and then assembling other entertainment assets that both support and draw value from the characters and images in those films.

The power of Walt's "integration" theory was perhaps most vividly revealed following his death. Within 15 years of that time, leadership at Disney seemed to lose sight of that vision.

As the company's films markedly shifted away from the core capability of animation, the engine of value creation ground to a halt. Film revenues declined. Gate receipts at Disneyland flattened. Character licensing slipped. *The Wonderful World of Disney*, the TV show that American families had gathered to watch every Sunday evening, in a nationwide embrace, was dropped from network broadcast. By the late 1970s, the Disney franchise many of us had grown to love as children had all but disappeared.

Attesting to the depths of Disney's disarray was when the unthinkable happened, an attempted hostile takeover of the company. But Michael Eisner and Frank Wells, who deeply believed in Walt Disney's vision, rode to the rescue. Once onboard, they would re-invigorate "integration" in the company to become Hollywood's most synergy-minded organization. And I was to play a key role in making it work.

The creation of a formal synergy program at Disney was initially handled by Art Levitt, a young executive that Eisner had drafted into service. Levitt also served as Eisner and Wells' executive assistant overseeing a new Disney department called Corporate Marketing. After just a few years in that role, Levitt relocated to Florida after he was offered a senior position to oversee an entertainment, dining, and retail area called Pleasure Island at Walt Disney World. While Levitt had begun formulating a synergy process at the company, Disney was really just dipping its toe into the synergy waters at that time.

In 1989, they hired Linda Warren, a razor-sharp and seasoned Disney marketing executive who took over Levitt's dual positions. It was her charge to up the synergy game. Eisner and Wells had become familiar with Warren when she and her boss, Walt Disney World Marketing chief Tom Elrod, met with them soon after their arrival at Disney. Warren said, "When Michael and Frank came onboard in 1984, they saw completely untapped resources within the company. One of which was Walt Disney World where I was then working under Tom Elrod who headed marketing there at that time."

At Elrod and Warren's first meeting with the new Disney leaders they were immediately challenged by the pair. "They said, "We want you to come up with a hundred ideas of how you're going to accelerate marketing at Walt Disney World."

And that tall order had a few more caveats. "They also wanted us to get a million-and-a-half additional visitors in the current year. Plus, in ten days they were traveling to Walt Disney World and wanted us to present everything they asked for."

Tom and Linda headed the team who did indeed come up with the 100 ideas requested. Warren recalled, "At the top of the list was expanding our advertising in various markets. Plus Michael and Frank were pleasantly surprised with what the team put together in all the ideas, the result of which was that we actually upped the visitor goal by a million and a half that year. I knew from that point on, nothing would ever be the same."

Warren admitted that it was truly marketing magician Elrod's leadership who took them to that goal.

Before being offered the corporate by position by Eisner and Wells in 1989, earlier in that same year Warren had been promoted to director of Marketing at Walt Disney World, a job she was very excited about taking on.

But just three months into that position she got a call from Dick Nunis, then president of Walt Disney Attractions, who told her that Michael and Frank were interested in having her relocate to California to replace Art Levitt. She was very reluctant to leave her marketing "dream job", but agreed to interview with them. She got the job. Although it meant leaving her new marketing role at Walt Disney World, she realized that working at the Disney corporate headquarters in California with the CEO and president of the company was a once-in-a-lifetime opportunity. "They were really, really focused on synergy. Art Levitt had begun the synergy surge, but as Michael said, "I now want to put a full court press on it and have you handle that responsibility."

This all was happening as I was starting to think about leaving Disneyland. In 1990, I made a cold call to Linda Warren and spoke to her about my interest in returning to Burbank. I knew Linda in passing since she had been on the Walt Disney World marketing team for many years before accepting her senior executive role at the studio a year earlier. It was the right phone call at the right time. She was seeking a new communications person to get onboard the synergy machine that she, Michael, and Frank were building. I was hired as manager of Corporate Synergy and Special Projects, the new name for what had been Corporate Marketing. Ultimately, I was promoted to director while Linda rose to become VP of the department.

Eisner loved the "s" word. In fact, in his book *Great Partnerships*, he remarked that "Frank and I were maniacal about synergy". And they were. In their view, every priority project for the company had synergy potential.

Warren soon began turning up the synergy heat to create a broader methodology to intensify company cross-promotions. My role in the mix was to develop a systematic communications program to keep the right hand knowing what the left hand was doing throughout all 60 or so independent Disney business segments so that each could take advantage of all possible synergy opportunities.

Corporate profits, of course, are at the heart of working synergy in any organization. Beginning in the 1970s, companies began gobbling up other companies. Diversification under one corporate umbrella was growing at a rapid pace, especially through the 1990s and into the new century.

The opportunities for cross-promoting from within were mind-boggling, and yet incorporating a synergy component to company-wide marketing strategies remained mostly unsupported in corporate America. That is, until Michael Eisner and Frank Wells got control of Disney.

In today's world, ten mega-corporations control the output of almost everything you buy from household products to pet food to jeans. According to the mic.com (a hard news site targeted to millennials), Yum Brands owns KFC and Taco Bell. The company was a spin-off of Pepsi. All Yum Brands restaurants sell only Pepsi products because of a special partnership with the soda-maker.

Eighty-four-billion-dollar company Proctor & Gamble, the largest advertiser in the U.S., is paired with a number of diverse brands that produce everything from medicine to toothpaste to high-end fashion. All tallied, P&G reportedly serves a whopping 4.8 billion people around the world through their network.

Two-hundred-billion-dollar corporation Nestle—famous for chocolate, but the biggest food company in the world—owns nearly 8,000 different brands worldwide and takes stake in or is partnered with many others.

Included in this network: shampoo company L'Oreal, baby food giant Gerber, clothing brand Diesel, and pet food makers Purina and Friskies. Unilever, of soap fame, reportedly serves two billion people globally, controlling a network that produces everything from Q-tips to Skippy peanut butter.

Control of the media arena in which Disney resides today is controlled by just five companies down from 50 companies in 1983. They are: Time Warner with notable properties that include: HBO, Time Inc. Turner Broadcasting System, Warner Bros. Entertainment, TMZ, New Line Cinema, Time Warner Cable, Cinemax, Cartoon Network, TBS (Turner Broadcasting System), TNT (Turner Network Television), America Online, MapQuest, Moviefone, Castle Rock, Sports Illustrated, Fortune, Marie Clair and People Magazine; The Walt Disney Company owning Disney/ABC Television Group, ABC Television Network, ABC Family, Disney Channels Worldwide, ESPN, Walt Disney Studios Motion Pictures, Walt Disney Animation Studios, Pixar Animation Studios, Disney Music Group, Disney Theatrical Group, DisneyToon Studios, Marvel Studios, Touchstone Pictures, Disneynature, Disney Publishing Worldwide, and Disney Interactive, among others.

Viacom has MTV Films, Nickelodeon, Paramount Animation, Paramount Pictures, BET (Black Entertainment Network), CMT (Country Music Television), Comedy Central, Logo Network, MTV, Nick at Nite, Nick Jr., Spike, TV Land, and VH1; NewsCorp. owns 20th Century Fox Filmed Entertainment, Fox Broadcasting Company, MyNetworkTV, Fox Sports Networks, FX Networks, National Geographic Channel, *The Sun* and *The Times UK* newspapers, The *New York Post*, *Wall Street Journal*, *Barron's*, MarketWatch, *Financial News*, Dow Jones news wires, and HarperCollins.

And lastly, Comcast Corporation that counts among its holdings two primary businesses, Comcast Cable and NBCUniversal. Comcast Cable is the nation's largest video, high-speed Internet and phone provider to residential customers under the XFINITY brand and also provides these services to businesses. NBCUniversal operates news, entertainment and sports cable networks, the NBC and Telemundo broadcast networks, television production operations and television station groups, Universal Pictures and Universal Parks and Resorts.

These five giants control a staggering 90% of what we read, listen to, or watch.

Some additional facts related to the Big Five, as compiled by *Business Insider*:

- A total of 232 media executives control the information diet of 277 million Americans.
- Total revenue in 2010 for the Big Five was $275.9 billion; that's $36 billion more than Finland's gross domestic product, enough to buy every NFL team 12 times, and five times the government bailout of

General Motors.

- The Big Five control 70% of cable programming and one of every five hours of television overall, and their 2010 box-office sales hit $7 billion—that's twice the box-office sales of the next 140 studios combined.

These are very powerful statistics that offer so much opportunity to synergize across business units. But is synergy a "priority" within these organizations?

Of course, the urge to merge and acquire more corporate assets points to dollars, Big Dollars, generated to elevate the bottom line and to make investors willing, if not eager, to pay higher prices for shares in the company's stock.

In turn, the conglomerate attains more assets and, if successful, renews the process again and again, ever expanding its horizons. But with each new acquisition, more often than not, the company becomes more decentralized with no common distinction. If divisions don't relate in product or services, Business A doesn't deal with Business B, or Business C with Business D, even though they all fall under the umbrella of the parent company. Yet the success factor can still be amazing.

But, how much more successful might they be if they were able to better utilize their internal forces to cross-promote from *within*, to stimulate overall business *in addition* to each faction meeting individual goals? Even in a single-focused operation, does the research and development department ever speak with the accounting folks, or does the marketing department dialogue with the sales division? Do the creative people spend any time with the operations force? More simplistically, does the person in the next cubicle converse over the partition about the company or how they might use their knowledge together to generate something even greater than each could accomplish alone?

Within organizations, boundaries exist between levels of the corporation and across departmental and geographic lines. While there are some good reasons for structuring organizations this way, strict adherence to boundaries can inhibit collaboration and have profound impacts on an organization's success or failure.

The question usually is, "What does my business, cruise ships (for example), have to do with book publishing, another company division?" Off the top of your head, you might think nothing. But put on your thinking cap. Here are some possibilities for working together and for cross-promotion for the greater benefit of both divisions:

- Have a special "author's cruise" and include top writers from the Publishing division to participate in an entertaining Q&A session with travelers as well as having book signings.

- Market special cruises to vacationers through book clubs and through bookstores, probably an untapped resource for the cruise division.
- Have the Publishing division develop a book on "Cruising" using their own company cruise line as the ultimate example of luxury vacationing, then sell the book onboard.

It's really not hard, it's just getting that line of communication open.

Working synergy at Disney literally meant being "inside the heart of the Disney marketing machine". We who worked at synergy every day have never shared the techniques and strategies employed to bring it to the success it became at Disney, mostly because we kept our processes close to the vest. However, more than a quarter century has passed, and how we worked synergy in the Eisner and Wells era is clearly a part of Disney history. Since that time, we've all moved on to new challenges and, of course, Michael Eisner is no longer the corporate face of Disney and Frank Wells, sadly, has passed away.

The bottom line about synergy isn't that a diversified company will be unsuccessful without enabling it within their organization; certainly, corporations that are not synergy focused are very profitable. But making the most of synergy gives diverse companies a calculable *edge*. It is, in fact, marketing from the inside out, and when implemented correctly can skyrocket mediocrity to success, and success to mega-victory. But it does take an organized plan of action, a step-by-step process.

Through that process, so many Disney projects were elevated to higher levels than might ever have been achieved without the cross-promotional support and cooperation of Disney businesses that were not the division initiating the project but were supporting it in numerous ways through their own marketing. As Michael Eisner has said so many times back in the day, "At Disney, 1 + 1 = 3." That's synergy.

CHAPTER SEVENTEEN

The Big Picture View

During my tenure in Synergy at The Walt Disney Company there were two basic origins of synergy projects. First, there were those that started from within a specific business unit. For example:

- *Aladdin* animated film, originating from Buena Vista Pictures
- Disneyland's 35th Anniversary, originating from Walt Disney Parks & Resorts
- Disney Cruise Line, originating from Walt Disney Parks & Resorts

Second, there were synergy projects that started as an overall "umbrella" campaign for the entire company, and were usually tied to a special anniversary, such as:

- Mickey's 60th Anniversary
- Donald Duck's 50th Anniversary
- The Walt Disney Company's 75th Anniversary

Many major synergy projects were actually a combination of the two— one business unit primarily drives the idea, but by its nature it will become a promotional umbrella for the entire company. The example of Disney acquiring the Mighty Ducks, an NHL Hockey team, in 1993 was just such a project. (The company sold the team in 2005.)

Not all events, films, TV shows, new product, etc. were considered synergy priorities that could permeate the company. We carefully focused on those that we considered had the characteristics of a great synergy project. Those traits included projects that lent themselves well to all or most Disney businesses in terms of cross-promotional opportunities. For example, "Disney branded" products or events were often a primary driver for its originating business unit, and perhaps most importantly, fostered a naturally occurring synergistic enthusiasm throughout the company. Keep in mind that synergy cannot be forced; it's like trying to fit a square peg into a round hole, and it just doesn't work that way.

Perhaps the best way to understand the process as it was implemented at Disney is to look at a few examples, some of which are "synergy-obvious" and others not so much.

Disney's 31st animated feature, *Aladdin*, from Walt Disney Pictures, was 1992's BIG priority and a perfect synergy project. The external marketing campaign was driven from the film's originating business segment, Buena Vista Pictures Marketing. Synergy became an internal marketing component of that campaign; it was the icing on the cake. Ultimately, this project produced an enormous array of synergies with nearly every Disney business unit participating. It was the perfect synergy project and a home run for the entire company. To give you a taste of the goings-on, the following are just a few of the cross-promotions that it inspired, including those involving Disney Corporate Alliance partner companies:

- Buena Vista Pictures held *Aladdin* promotional sweepstakes for trips to Disneyland and Disney World supported by Walt Disney Feature Animation, the Disney Store, Walt Disney World Resort, Disneyland Resort, The Disney Catalog, Walt Disney Records, Disney Computer Software, Disney Press, and Delta Air Lines.
- Buena Vista Pictures Distribution held nationwide in-theater contests.
- The Walt Disney Special Events Group produced a live show that was included with the film presentation of *Aladdin* at Hollywood's El Capital Theatre.
- Network TV Specials produced two one-hour TV specials on *The Best of Disney Music*, airing on CBS. Each program included a segment on *Aladdin*.
- Buena Vista Home Video added an *Aladdin* trailer on over 15 million *Beauty and the Beast* videocassettes. They also created an *Aladdin* Sing-Along.
- The Disney Channel aired a 30-minute special, *The Making of Aladdin*. They also created an *Aladdin* Magic Carpet Ride Sweepstakes.
- The Disney Channel Magazine provided editorial coverage of *Aladdin*.
- The Disneyland Resort showcased six *Aladdin* animated windows at the Emporium on Main Street, U.S.A. *Aladdin* walk-around characters began appearing in-park with the movie opening, soon followed by Aladdin's Royal Caravan Parade and Aladdin's Oasis restaurant.
- Walt Disney World supported *Aladdin* with poster kiosks and Emporium windows, while the Disney-MGM Studios support included poster displays, tram cards, guidebooks, and animation displays. A segment on *Aladdin* was included in the nationally televised Walt

Disney World Christmas Parade.

- Disney Publishing released a slate of *Aladdin* books including flip books, illustrated classics, junior novelizations, pop-up books, and coffee table book detailing the making of the movie.

- *Disney Adventures* magazine featured *Aladdin* on the cover with a two-part "making of" story inside.

- Disney Publishing, Comics, came out with an *Aladdin* Graphic Novel, *Aladdin* Cartoon Tales, an *Aladdin* Junior Graphic Novel, and *Aladdin* mini-comics suitable for promotional use.

- Disney Consumer Products Licensing launched a huge array of *Aladdin* product including a wide range of children's wearables. Retail programs were showcased at Walmart, K-Mart, Venture, JC Penney, Toys "R" Us, Mervyn's, May Company, and Bloomingdale's. Eight licensees participated in a Disney Adventures *Aladdin* sweepstakes. T-shirts and board games featured as self-liquidating offers on the back of eleven million boxes of Cap'N Crunch Cereal.

- Walt Disney Art Classics produced *Aladdin* limited-edition serigraphs and hand-drawn animation cels, in addition to limited-edition porcelain sculptures at an auction at Sotheby's in New York City of production artwork from the film.

- The Disney Store featured an enormous array of *Aladdin* licensed and exclusive product. *Aladdin* windows were featured in all U.S./Canada stores. *Aladdin* movie clips were included in the corporate loop that ran in every store. A feature article was run in the Disney Store Credit Card newsletter. Cast member *Aladdin* buttons worn in-store, and an *Aladdin* promo was printed on every register receipt.

- Walt Disney Records released an *Aladdin* soundtrack, *Aladdin* Read-Along Collection, *Aladdin* Sound and Story Theater, and *Aladdin* Deluxe Read-Along with Pop-Ups.

- Disney Software launched the *Aladdin* Print Kit.

Aladdin was the most successful film of 1992, grossing $218 million in the United States and over $504 million worldwide. It was the biggest gross for an animated film until Disney's *The Lion King* two years later. It also won two Academy Awards, for Best Music, Original Score, and Best Music, Original Song, for "A Whole New World".

Hollywood Records, a non-Disney branded "adult" label business unit, is an example of a division that did not lend itself well to synergy efforts or support. It had no obvious Disney tie-in or Disney character fit. In the case of this division, the key was to find the "hook" that other business units could "hang" a product or project on, or to recognize select businesses that could participate in a synergy program instead of all businesses, as illustrated by the *Aladdin* example.

But we did find a way. In June 1990, Hollywood Records acquired the music catalog of the legendary rock band Queen in the United States and Canada. With that acquisition, they put together a marketing plan including advertising, consumer marketing, and sales. And then a little synergy kicked in. One Queen hit, "We Will Rock You", had become an anthem of sorts at hockey games around the nation. Disney released a film focusing on hockey called *The Mighty Ducks* in 1992. Part of the song "We Will Rock You" was used in the movie's soundtrack and Hollywood Records retro-released a "We Will Rock You" video that featured footage from *The Mighty Ducks* movie.

"We Will Rock You" found its way to Disney's Mighty Ducks NHL team (named for the film) where the song was played at every game. Additionally, from a synergy standpoint, Queen music was played nightly at Pleasure Island, an area that is no longer around, but was once a nighttime entertainment district at Walt Disney World. The Queen music catalog was also for sale there.

All of the above are fine examples of how working synergy within a diversified company can produce over-the-top results and huge corporate profits. But exactly how do you get everyone to play the game to produce such impressive outcomes?

CHAPTER EIGHTEEN

It Starts at the Top

When I stepped into my new role in Synergy, I must admit, I had no clue where to start. There was no roadmap for how to work synergy inside a massive conglomerate like Disney; we were starting a brand-new process. I was baffled. For about the first six months on the job, I struggled to wrap my head around how it would all work, trying this and that. But then I had an "aha" moment that clarified everything in my mind.

Very simply, my career at Disney prior to this point had been as a PR executive. It suddenly occurred to me that many of the same strategies I had used to promote Disney projects to the media *outside* the company could be put into place to promote synergy *inside* the company. I likened my role to communicating with the media, but instead I would converse with Disney marketing, entertainment, and creative decision-makers with news about the company that served their business interests.

In other words, to me a synergy department was akin to an internal publicity department. The difference was that I would be promoting the company to the company vs. promoting a film, TV show, or event to the outside world. What a concept! It was the trigger that opened my eyes as to how to proceed forward. Corporate Synergy and Special Projects would serve as an in-house agency to the rest of the company.

If I was PR savvy (and I am), then I was also synergy savvy and so was everyone else going to be...at least on my watch. And remember, it was all done at a time when procedures and communication were very low-tech. The internet was in its infancy. Few people had cell phones. There was no such thing as texting or widespread use of digital files, and certainly no social media of any kind. Facebook, Twitter, Instagram, LinkedIn, and all digital conversational tools that promote communication were "of the future".

To get the synergy ball rolling, I first compiled a database of internal synergy constituents, primarily marketing, entertainment, and creative executives company-wide that would be the receivers of all synergy communications. Marketing executives are a good choice since they lead the charge to shape public perception of the company through their own divisions and products.

I included manager level and above on the roster. These are executives who can make independent decisions in the life of a given project. I also included all the most senior staff in the company, along with the CEO, on the distribution as well. The database started small, but continued to grow as the synergy process grew. In order to always have the list be current, it was important for me to keep apprised of newly incoming key executives as well as those who left the company.

Then, I worked my way through several iterations of a communications program before a final process was approved. The first idea to spread the synergy news was to create a newsletter that I titled *In the Loop*. That idea was rejected because by the time information was gathered to place in the newsletter, the news would be old. Then I presented *In the Loop* to my boss as a kind of press release vs. a newsletter. That idea was rejected because Eisner didn't think it was business-like enough. As Linda Warren remarked to me at the time, "We're getting closer."

The next communications concept was the winner. It was called Synergy News and utilized the standard Disney inter-office memo stationary, but with the addition of the words "Synergy News" affixed in a red font to the top right-hand corner of the letterhead. It was a business-like simple identity. But I wasn't quite satisfied. I thought it needed just a little bit more.

It was then that I also decided that my communications not only needed words per the Synergy News identity to set them apart, but also something more tangible. Thinking as a PR person, I felt we needed a "brand" to make synergy real.

Unfortunately, synergy is not something you can pick up and hold in your hand. Nor can you take it for a ride in your car or put it on your desk as a paperweight. And if it's not real, who's going to believe it will work? So, we needed to attach a face to the concept to enforce that it was an actual function in the company. In my experience, the best way to do that was to create a logo and attach it to every document that went out from the Corporate Synergy office. Circulation of the logo across divisions on a regular basis would make synergy a very real corporate function.

We then engaged an outside graphic design firm that I had worked with many times in my PR career to create a Disney Synergy logo. The image consisted of three "gear-turning" circles to make the simple image of Mickey Mouse's head. Eisner and Warren quickly approved it for internal use only, as no synergy communications were ever distributed outside of the company at that time. Synergy News became the first communication vehicle to showcase our new "brand". But there were certainly more branded communications to come.

At the top of the list for synergy success at Disney was, of course, to have the CEO driving the concept. Eisner and Wells had to be viewed by company executives as the true captains of the synergy ship. Without their ongoing leadership and drive to incorporate synergy into the very fabric of the company, it would never have worked as well as it did. Movers and shakers in a company are always reluctant to play ball unless they know Big Brother is watching. Therefore, the very first synergy communication that was distributed from my office was one that laid out the expectations.

A directive was composed that came directly from Michael Eisner in the form of a inter-office memo distributed to a compiled list of marketing, entertainment, and creative executives; all of his direct reports; and the company's entire senior staff. The memos were individually addressed to each person on the list, and Michael personally signed each and every one of a mailing that totaled about 500 key individuals at that time. This was our first important synergy communication and, above all, we wanted it to be taken seriously.

The following is the inter-office memo, dated January 25, 1991, that was distributed:

> In an effort to establish the highest level of awareness for synergy opportunities within The Walt Disney Company, beginning in early 1991, the Corporate Synergy and Special Projects Department will begin a regular and ongoing distribution of internal Synergy News Memos designed to disperse timely information on significant company projects across all businesses.

> With the size, scope and diversity of our company, a tremendous need exists for all of us to keep abreast of our full and ongoing slate of activities. Synergy is part of what makes our company the success it is today and Frank and I are on the Synergy Detail. We believe the Synergy News Memos are a great way to start the communication ball rolling across the company and to maintain ongoing communication, in writing, for you to use as reference in your planning process.

> Focusing on one source topic, each Synergy News Memo will report on company-wide activities in motion, those in development and in discussion, as well as additional ideas for broader reach. Specific contacts from the originating business unit and from the Corporate Synergy and Special Projects Department will be listed on each memo for your information and use. Distribution will be company-wide, domestically and internationally, to marketing executives as well as to other appropriate internal recipients. Since synergy information is being distributed to enable you to work programs into your planning process at an early stage, as well as generate overall awareness on a timely basis, some topic details may be tentative; however, updates will be released as soon as the information is available.

The Corporate Synergy and Special Projects Department will prepare all Synergy News Memos and distribute the information. All divisional marketing meetings with the various business units will be overseen by Linda Warren and she will report regularly on the synergistic progress of each project to all the business unit heads at my regular staff meetings.

Current Synergy News Memos in process include "The Disney Afternoon Live" at Disneyland, emanating from Attractions and Resorts (although synergistically spun-off from Buena Vista TV's syndicated *Duck Tales*, *Gummi Bears*, *Rescue Rangers*, and *TaleSpin*); "The Disney Adventures" from Publishing;, "Queen", from Hollywood Records; "Disney Clubs", from Buena Vista International Television; "The Second Annual American Teacher Awards Special", from The Disney Channel; and "1992, The Year of Goofy", among others.

Although the best way to accomplish synergy is via one-on-one communication with and between the members of each of the business units, it is my hope that this new internal communication will enhance overall synergy efforts throughout The Walt Disney Company.

Michael Eisner

This first directive got synergy off to the right start. Before long, Synergy News memos began to flow out to our database. We were to be positioned as the in-the-know, close-to-the-top providers of internal company information to the movers and shakers of the organization.

However, the Disney marketers had plenty on their plates to keep them busy without further dictates from Corporate Synergy, and no marketing, entertainment, or creative executive in the company reported to us. We couldn't force them to participate in any project. We had to use motivational tactics, not command-or-dictate rules to get them to play synergy ball. In fact, it went further: we had to generate excitement along with information. Over time, with much work on building relationships, everything we threw at them to spark new synergy partnerships grew to bonfire levels.

The entire process became exactly what Eisner and Wells had hoped it could be. They never could understand why other big companies did not embrace a well-crafted synergy methodology. When someone once asked Eisner why Time Warner had not been able to make synergy work, he responded, "You want the one-minute or four-hour answer?" He settled on the one-minute reply: "It all comes down to company DNA. I simply stressed that every division had to work with every other one. We had a brand, and the Disney brand had to work through every business unit. If Time Warner doesn't do it...they're losing out. Walt Disney was the most synergistic guy of all time."

CHAPTER NINETEEN

Disney Dimensions

One of Linda Warren's first synergy directives, and one that she considers one of her most successful on the path to foster synergy throughout the company, was the development of a program called Disney Dimensions.

As Michael Eisner described in a 2000 interview with the *Harvard Business Review*: "First and foremost, making synergy happen began with the Disney Dimensions program. We ran the program once or twice a year for about twenty-five senior executives from every division of the company worldwide. It was like a synergy boot camp."

Indeed it was. The executive participants went through eight to ten days of meetings covering every aspect of the company. They spent several days in California, in Burbank at the company headquarters and Walt Disney Animation Studios, in Glendale at Walt Disney Imagineering, and in Anaheim at The Disneyland Resort. They then moved on to Walt Disney World in Florida and to New York where Disney Publishing, Disney Theatrical (Broadway productions), and ABC/Cap Cities and ESPN (acquired in 1996) are based. Included were intensive meetings with key executives at each location.

During the nearly two-week endeavor, they spent time with motion-picture executives, the legal department, corporate finance, and with human resources to understand the values of the company. They experienced presentations from every division of the company, from Animation, Film and Television, Research and Development, and Consumer Products, to Theatrical Productions and Film Distribution, Parks and Resorts... everything.

And then more experiences were incorporated into their Disney Dimensions agenda, most of which were not what is usually found on a senior-level executive's calendar. Eisner explained, "Everyone experienced portraying a Disney performer in the parks, they heard how you cook 10,000 meals a day, they saw how the beds are made at our hotels, they learned what it's like to work in 100-degree heat and 100% humidity, to clean bathrooms, cut hedges, check guests out of a hotel, and soothe tired children."

The Disney Dimensions attendees started each day at 7:00 am and went straight through to 11 pm. While on the program, they were not allowed to do "regular" business. Attention was focused on the tasks at hand.

The group was together all day and all night, other than getting a much-needed good night's sleep. Despite the workload, their company march was made very comfortable. Attendees were flown to the various Disney locations on a company jet, and they enjoyed wonderful meals and being housed at the best hotels during the trip. But it did take lots of stamina. Eisner said, "Believe me, everyone started off dreading Disney Dimensions. But by the third day, they loved it, and by the end, they have totally bonded. They've learned to respect what tens of thousands of people do, and they become friends at the same time. When they went back to their jobs, what happened was synergy...naturally."

Disney Dimensions participants soon found themselves phoning their boot camp mates (remember, no tweets or texts then) to discuss cross-promotional opportunities on a regular basis. "It was truly an immersion program that had spectacular results," said Linda Warren.

While Disney Dimensions had put Warren on the path to making important synergistic inroads in the company, she also felt, "We still needed to hit on all cylinders to make sure we got information to all layers of the company, not just the senior executives. And we needed to do so on an ongoing basis."

It was then that Warren decided to hire a synergy communications person to push out material to mid-level marketing and entertainment executives throughout the company. They were indeed the worker bees that could make things happen at that level, and their involvement would then transmit information vertically both up and down the organization. It was the perfect complement to what was already happening to foster synergy at the most senior level of the company.

In that regard, Linda worked tirelessly with upper management on a daily basis to follow-through on the synergy status of each Eisner directive. "Michael's Monday Lunch" was where much of the cross-promotional discussions took place. The weekly meeting was attended by the heads of each Disney business unit, Warren, and all of Eisner's direct reports. Warren said, "These were team get-togethers that happened faithfully every Monday where the heads of the divisions each talked about each other's businesses. It was largely a synergy meeting in that we monitored how the businesses were working together, how could we make a particular film open even stronger, how could we make an attraction even more important, how can we help Consumer Products. The bottom line was how could the company bring all its resources to bear on things that would not only benefit shareholders, but also make everything bigger than they ordinarily would if everyone was just working in their own silos. I do think this was the key that many companies still don't get."

Warren traveled all over the world with Eisner and Wells, and got to see how their relationship matured and developed: "They wouldn't be together all the time, but they would be so enthusiastic about recapping each other's day, what they did, what decisions had been made, and with whom they met. It was a wonderful thing to watch just how genuinely they got along and how excited they were about all the prospects for the company. Also, they treated everyone with a lot of respect."

Warren remembered a particular moment early on when she gained insight into Eisner's behavior. "It was my first trip with Michael and it was just the two of us traveling to Milan. I brought way too much stuff and had multiple suitcases. Upon getting our bags, I thought perhaps I should pick up some of his bags along with my own. He quickly jumped in and said, "Oh, don't be ridiculous, give me the bags." He was so nice and Frank was, too. They were both tough when they needed to be, but they were also very kind."

In all the time she worked so closely with Eisner and Wells, she never saw them say a cross word to each other.

At the top levels of the company, Warren enjoyed getting to know Michael's executive team as well and was a big fan of Studio chief, Jeffrey Katzenberg. "Jeffrey was always great to me, and was legendary about keeping in touch with people for years and years. I was on his call list and he would check in with me all the time and that meant a lot to me."

Katzenberg was known to be a workaholic. He often arrived at the studio so early in the morning it was still dark outside. At the end of the day he left on the same basis and expected those who reported to him to maintain a similar schedule. Jeffrey's reputation resulted in a phrase allegedly attributed to him: "If you don't come in on Saturday, don't bother coming in on Sunday." He was absolutely driven to revitalize Disney in the filmmaking arena, especially when it came to animated product.

Under the leadership of Roy E. Disney, Chairman of Feature Animation, Katzenberg put in endless hours with the artists, writers, producers, and directors that created *Beauty and the Beast*, *Aladdin*, and *The Lion King*, all smash hits. He also oversaw Disney's television arm, generating such long-running series as *The Golden Girls* and *Home Improvement*.

While I didn't have direct interaction with Katzenberg, my work in synergy was often all about fostering cross-promotions for Disney animated movies, always a company priority. So many of the Disney business units needed to support almost everything that Roy E. Disney and Katzenberg would initiate.

I remember when I first came on board, Linda put out a memo to all key executives in the company explaining what my role was to be. In it she wrote: "Lorraine will be instrumental in developing a systematic plan to establish an ongoing awareness of synergistic activities company-wide." It seemed clear to me. But not everyone agreed.

Linda received the memo back from a senior management executive in Imagineering (who shall remain nameless) who had sarcastically written on it in red pen: "...if Lorraine can explain this sentence [underlining 'developing a systematic plan to establish an ongoing awareness of synergistic activities company-wide'], she'll be a total success!"

It took some time, but indeed the system that was ultimately developed did establish an ongoing awareness through a variety of creative, and often fun, approaches. Breaking down silos, team building, idea sharing, exploring possibilities, generating momentum, fostering enthusiasm, advancing the ball, cultivating a synergy culture, and so much more were all part of the Synergy department's mission. But it wasn't simple and took far more thought, trial and error, highs and lows, to establish internally than I ever could have imagined. But it did work; in fact, it worked like a well-oiled Disney marketing machine.

CHAPTER TWENTY

Communicate, Communicate, Communicate

Making synergy work at Disney was all about building relationships and incorporating solid communication principles into the mix. Education, communication, and motivation were used to fire up the corporate audience on a timely and regular basis, although we had no set timetable on when to distribute material. But when we did, it was very thorough.

For example, generically speaking, if a project were to involve the development of a new light bulb as a key priority for the company overall, everything about that light bulb, from the idea to the research to the packaging to the marketing plan had to be shared with the total audience in order to generate their enthusiasm and support. They had to be included in the process right from the get-go. If they saw synergy opportunities for their business, they would take ownership of the project, too.

To give you an idea of the flavor of one of our communications, the following sample features information contained in an early Synergy News Memo. The subject was Walt Disney World's 20th Anniversary:

> On October 1, 1991, Walt Disney World will launch an exciting 14-month celebration (October 1991–December 1992) to commemorate its 20th anniversary, under the banner theme, "The World's Most Spectacular Surprise!" A high-profile event, the 20th anniversary will offer numerous synergistic opportunities for many Disney businesses.
>
> On February 14, Walt Disney World presented its overall slate of activities to executives within the Studio and Consumer Products business units. Following are the key marketing and entertainment elements in development:
>
> **Magic Kingdom**
> *Surprise Daytime Parade*: Every day, Walt Disney World will surprise a guest and honor him/her by making them grand marshal of the new 20th Anniversary Parade. The parade will be internationally themed

and feature 35 ft. Disney character inflatables. The primary character focus of the parade will be Roger Rabbit.

New Evening Attraction: Electro-Magic Surprise, the innovative, technologically advanced and state-of-the-art nighttime attraction will debut. The parade will be fiber-optically lit and include twelve Electro-Magic characters.

Surprise Giveaways: Promotional items will be given to guests at the Diamond Horseshoe Jamboree, Tomorrowland Theater, Mickey's Starland, and the Castle Forecourt.

Disney/MGM Studios

Premier of Muppet 3-D Movie during 20th Anniversary press event (9/28/91–10/1/91). The film will have a soft opening in Spring 1991.

Mickey's Magic Show: Replacing the Dick Tracy Stage Show at the Hollywood Bowl Theater, Mickey's Magic Show will feature surprise/illusion elements.

Surprise Giveaways: Promotional items will be given to guests at the Theater of the Stars, Superstar Television, Monster Sound Show, and the Indiana Jones Stunt Show pre-show.

EPCOT Center

Surprise Daytime Fireworks and Aerial Show: The daytime display will be billed as the world's largest daytime fireworks show. Added entertainment will be fun-filled aerial displays with Disney performers and characters flying in motorized parachutes.

Surprise Giveaways: Promotional items will be given to EPCOT guests at the American Gardens.

A second-tier focus to the overall event will be the "Disney Past Guest" salute, designed to bring anyone who ever visited Walt Disney World in the past 20 years back to visit during the 14-month celebration. There will be a major publicity campaign and "worldwide search" for 80 million people via classified ads in major newspapers around the world, among other promotionally oriented pursuits. An incentive plan to bring back past guests tentatively includes:

- Honorary homecoming ceremonies
- Honored guest "Citizen of the World" status with special park privileges
- On-site recognition with homecoming names posted in special locations
- Special offers for "past guest" resort packages
- Early admissions to Parks

Plans are also in development for promotional "Surprise" target market tours, travel agent "Surprise" party kits, and "Surprise" public relations efforts that include "Surprise" character visits to hospitals, schools, etc.

To launch the entire celebration, Walt Disney World will host an international media event, tentatively scheduled from Sept. 28 to Oct. 1, 1991. Proposed highlights in development include:

- Ceremony commemorating 20 years of Walt Disney World
- Premier of *Muppet 3-D* film to include dedication ceremonies and press conference
- Walt Disney World salute to the 50th Anniversary of the USO
- Celebration honoring "Points of Light"
- EPCOT Center Soviet Pavilion announcement
- Around-the-Clock "20 Years of Magic" Party

During the week of February 25, we will be scheduling meetings with appropriate Disney businesses to discuss synergy efforts on behalf of Walt Disney World's 20th Anniversary. As you can see, per the ideas in development, the scope of this event is huge, with endless opportunities for synergy company-wide.

Should you have any questions prior to the meetings, synergy contacts include:

Linda Warren, Corporate Synergy and Special Projects

Lorraine Santoli, Corporate Synergy and Special Projects

Elizabeth Schar, Walt Disney World Marketing

Attached to the memo was the complete list of the executives on the synergy distribution list who each received the informative communication. I wanted everyone receiving our documents to know who else was receiving them to further foster communication among those in the database.

I remember another Synergy News Memo that set a very fundamental basis for a new division of the company. In December 1992, Disney acquired an NHL (National Hockey League) franchise, then yet unnamed.

Immediately after the deal was sealed, I sent out a Synergy News Memo to our database releasing the acquisition information, but more importantly explaining to our synergy team everything there was to know, generically, about the game of hockey: How is the game played? How many men are on a team? How many divisions of the NHL are there? How many teams make up those divisions? What is the object of the game? What happens in the playoffs? What does the winning team take home? What are the demographics of hockey fans? What is their income level? I included everything our synergy partners would need to know because I wanted them to be fully prepared to start thinking about cross-promoting with the new team and their own business units. Educating them was the best way to begin.

As for naming the team, coming soon after the acquisition, Eisner jumped right in with his choice. He wanted to name the team "The Mighty Ducks" after the Disney film of the same name, a great crossover idea. But he faced lots of executive opposition. On March 3, 1993, the *Los Angeles Times* reported:

> Eisner is adamant in defending his plan to adopt the name of Disney's hit movie that starred Emilio Estevez as coach of a youth hockey team called The Mighty Ducks to Disney's new NHL franchise. Despite a lukewarm reception, Eisner said that The Mighty Ducks is the "front-runner and there is no second choice".

Not surprisingly, the NHL team was officially named The Mighty Ducks. The new acquisition became the first tenant of the Anaheim Arena (later named the Arrowhead Pond and now the Honda Center), a brand-new stadium located a short distance east of Disneyland. The venue was completed the same year the team was founded. In 2003 (a year prior to the team being sold by Disney), The Mighty Ducks came within a game of achieving Stanley Cup glory.

Early on, we also had to educate the synergy populace about the Corporate Synergy and Special Projects Department itself. We started by devising a mission statement:

> The Corporate Synergy and Special Projects Department will serve as a "center-link" service department to all internal divisions of The Walt Disney Company by providing key support functions—knowledge, communication, motivation, and camaraderie—in order to maximize synergy and drive overall company business to higher growth and profit levels.

Putting my publicist cap back on, I likened familiarizing our database with the role of Corporate Synergy role in the same way I would have prepared media with information on a new movie. We needed a press kit. But in this case, the "press kit" became a Corporate Synergy "Information Kit" that would be distributed internally to the synergy database.

In today's world, everything would be created online, but when I put the Corporate Synergy Information Kit together, it mirrored the classic PR press kit of old with a printed folder that featured the Corporate Synergy logo, in color, on the front, and when opened, featured a pocket on the right and left sides of the folder containing images inserted on the left and documents inserted on the right.

Of course, just as with a typical press kit, the right-hand pocket was imprinted with the contact information, in this case for the Synergy department. All of the documentation in the kit displayed the Corporate Synergy logo. I set about writing the materials by spending time at the Walt Disney Archives to research any historical information tied to the topic that I could use. That was where I found the aforementioned 1958 *Wall Street Journal* article, "Dream, Diversify and Never Miss an Angle" that was so useful to establish a strong historical company link to synergy.

Discovering that article and the illustration that accompanied it formed the foundation for the Synergy Information Kit that was distributed to the entire synergy database and then some. In addition to including a copy of the *Wall Street Journal* article and chart, the information also included facts about the mission of the Corporate Synergy and Special Projects Department, Fact Sheets, samples of synergy communications, and anything needed to generate understanding the synergy concept as it applied to the company.

Also added was a newly designed tri-fold chart that opened to illustrate Disney synergy in the world of the 1990s using interconnected turning gears, each gear representing a different Disney business unit. Some gears were big like the one for Walt Disney Pictures, Disneyland, Walt Disney World, The Disney Channel, and Disney Consumer Products, and some were smaller such as those showcasing Buena Vista Home Video, Walt Disney Records, Disney Publishing, Walt Disney Art Classics, and Disney Internet Group, for example. They were all depicted as turning in unison.

Now that everyone knew what the Corporate Synergy and Special Projects Department was about, it was time to move forward with another piece targeted to the synergy masses.

CHAPTER TWENTY-ONE

Educating the Company About the Company

Despite its synergistic history, The Walt Disney Company, like most large corporations, certainly suffered a degree of divisional tunnel vision. Executives were fervently aware of the projects happening and in-development within their own business units, but how much did they really know about the goings-on and priorities in the other divisions?

At the time I started working in Synergy, I could not find one document that listed every business segment of The Walt Disney Company in one place. That sounds ridiculous now, but back then it didn't exist, at least not for the general rank-and-file of the company. I'm sure somewhere there was a corporate structure listing all working divisions, what divisions oversaw others, and so forth, but if it was there, it surely wasn't obvious.

I hunted down information about every company business segment wherever I could find it, and was astonished that there were business units I had no idea existed. And if I didn't know, neither did many others in my synergy database. How can anyone successfully win the game if they don't even know every player on the field? I had to fix that, and quickly, if this synergy thing was going to work. I decided to devise another communications vehicle, this time with an educational slant.

I had a small staff of four people at the time and we all put our heads together to figure out the best way to familiarize those in our synergy database with every business segment in the company. We not only wanted to illustrate the structure of the overall organization to them, but also provide an understanding of each division's mission.

Of course, everyone was keenly aware of the key business drivers in the Disney organization—Film and TV, Theme Parks, and Consumer Products, for example. But there were many smaller divisions that were important cogs in the Disney wheel that needed to be recognized as well. All internal marketers needed to understand the big picture first before diving in to see how we could weave cross-promotional opportunities throughout all company businesses, not just the obvious ones.

We might have just put together a list or chart outlining all the divisions, which ones reported to others, etc., but that felt very boring; something no one would read and something to be filed away for another day. No, we were all creative marketing folks, surely there was a better way...a Disney way.

After a few brainstorming sessions with my team, what we decided to do was create a pocket-sized printed booklet (slickly designed, I might add!) that featured a paragraph or two about every company business segment, dividing each within its proper structure within the organization.

We started by placing the synergy logo on the cover page. That was important to emphasize our branded identity so everyone would know who created what ultimately became a valuable informational resource. Then we titled the booklet, The Walt Disney Company OVERVIEW.

An important decision was made as to who would write the paragraph or two that described the mission of each division. I could have used the information I had pulled together myself, but I sensed the material should rightly come from the source, not from my pen. Therefore, I asked a key person in each division that was part of my database to please provide a mission statement describing their business unit so that each section came straight from the horse's mouth, not through my filter. Since it was a relatively simple task, the information began to flow into my office.

That brings up another important factor when practicing synergy and attempting to lead others down the same path. While my department was the communications hub for all the spokes in the Disney synergy wheel, we never presumed to know more about any business unit than those who worked within those units. After all, no Disney business segment reported to Corporate Synergy.

We could tell no business what to do or how to do it when it came to applying a synergy component to their marketing plans. We had to move the process along using motivation, education, communication, and relationship building, to grease the synergy wheels.

My department's role was to maintain a "big picture" focus, communicating and reporting on the key priorities. It did not mean getting involved in anyone's business; they are making the decisions, we were only providing the stimulus. We nudged, but never pushed.

As a department, we also needed to remain neutral in our dealings with all company segments, so as not be viewed as favoring just larger Disney businesses, despite that it was those business segments which, for the most part, drove the company marketing train. We positioned ourselves to be a neutral zone, kind of like Switzerland.

In that regard, we worked very hard to provide every business unit, big and small, with the same respect and attention. While the big guns often led the parade, the smaller business units had much to add to internal cross-promotions, even if it was just adding a packaging "burst" supporting the bigger project. Like a puzzle, every piece contributes to the whole... that's the idea.

Once compiled, The Walt Disney OVERVIEW booklet contained everything needed to provide a good "big picture" view of the organization and all its diversified parts. The following is a sample of how the information was arranged based on the hierarchical structure of The Walt Disney Company in the early 1990s.

All caps words indicate the overarching business division under which its reporting business units are listed. To best illustrate how this booklet was arranged, I've included the brief mission statements of the first few units that fell under The Walt Disney Studios' banner at that time.

THE WALT DISNEY STUDIOS—Theatrical Motion Pictures

Walt Disney Pictures

Motion pictures released under the "Walt Disney Pictures" label represent all Disney animated films as well as those live-action features that are G-rated and traditionally marketed to families and young children. Recent Walt Disney Pictures releases include *White Fang*, *The Rocketeer*, and *Beauty and the Beast*.

Touchstone Pictures

Touchstone Pictures was created in 1984 to enable Disney to release features that are PG, PG-13 or R rated, with a more broad-based audience appeal. Recent releases from Touchstone Pictures include *Pretty Woman*, *What About Bob?*, and *Father of the Bride*.

Hollywood Pictures

Hollywood Pictures was established in 1987 to broaden the base of film releases from Disney. Recent releases include *The Hand that Rocks the Cradle* and *Medicine Man*.

Buena Vista Pictures Distribution

Buena Vista Pictures Distribution handles the distribution of motion-picture releases for Walt Disney Pictures, Touchstone Pictures, and Hollywood Pictures.

Buena Vista Pictures Marketing

Buena Vista Pictures Marketing handles the marketing of motion-picture releases for Walt Disney Pictures, Touchstone Pictures, and Hollywood Pictures.

Feature Animation

Producing animation for all Disney animated films and featurettes, the Animation Division of The Walt Disney Company has long been considered the entertainment industry leader in quality animation.

To date, Disney has produced 30 full-length animated feature films, from the release of *Snow White and the Seven Dwarfs* (1937) to *Beauty and the Beast* (1991). The newest full-length animated feature, set for a Christmas 1992 release, will be *Aladdin*.

To further enhance the layout of the booklet, we included logos for every division and, adding yet another dimension, we included sidebars on each page highlighting fun facts about the business units on that page. Some of the tidbits we included were placed on the appropriate pages to align with the proper business units:

> Through the years Walt Disney Pictures has been nominated for dozens of Academy Awards, winning a total of 66 competitive and special awards [up until that time].

> Walt Disney's first foray into series television, *Disneyland*, was aired under various titles for over thirty years, making it one of the longest-running television series in the history of the medium.

> In just 50 days, *Fantasia* became the #1 selling video of all time in North America, with total sales of 14,169,148 videocassettes and a record-breaking LaserDisc sale of 225,000 units.

> The Ingersoll Waterbury Company, makers of timepieces since 1856, had been pushed close to bankruptcy in the early 1930s when the firm was licensed to manufacture Mickey Mouse watches. Two-and-one-half-million Mickey Mouse watches were sold in two years.

> The horses on Disneyland's King Arthur Carrousel are 90–110 years old and are classic hand-carved and hand-painted mounts, with no two horses exactly alike.

> Disneyland guests buy in one year 4 million hamburgers, 1.6 million hot dogs, 3.4 million orders of fries, 3.2 million boxes of popcorn, 3.2 million servings of ice cream, and 1.2 gallons of soft drinks.

> At the peak of construction in 1970, Walt Disney World was the largest private construction project in the United States.

> Fifty-four million cubic feet of earth were moved to construct EPCOT Center.

> Disney's Contemporary Resort is the only hotel in the world to have a monorail run directly through its cavernous lobby concourse.

The booklet was compact (7"x4"), easy to carry around, and totaled just 23 short pages. But before going to print we had one more fun factor to add that was the icing on the booklet cake. It covered the entire inside back cover and, after reading about the mission and fun facts described within, further underscored the amazing scope of The Walt Disney Company.

The page was devised and written by Jeff Kurtti, a member of the Corporate Synergy staff at the time. Featured was a screened-back image of Mary Poppins holding a spoonful of sugar taken from the movie and covering the entire inside back page. Every item listed below emanated from a Walt Disney Company division. The text, layered over the Poppins image, read as follows:

A DISNEY "OUT-SICK" DAY

If you *have* to be out sick...once every ten years or so...

Of course, a loyal Disney employee (or just-plain Disney fanatic) wouldn't let something as trivial as a cold or 24-hour flu keep them from expanding their Disney horizons. Even as you lie around the house, there's plenty of Disney to keep you occupied:

8:00 am   Call your office—it's the right thing to do. Stay warm. Drink plenty of liquids. Curl up under your favorite comforter.

9:00 am   *LIVE! with Regis and Kathie Lee.* Light, fun, and entertaining. Just what the doctor ordered in terms of get-well distraction.

10:00 am   A good mystery book can really help you relax. Try Hyperion's *A Stained White Radiance*, by James Lee Burke. Intrigue and politics!

12:00 pm   Eat something. Chicken soup is everything it's claimed to be, recovery-wise. Skim through *Discover* magazine during lunch. Or how about *Family Fun* magazine? *Disney Adventures*? Okay, try Disney comics, they always make you feel better.

1:00 pm   Shouldn't you take a nap about now? If not, there's plenty of video to keep you occupied. Given your current health, how about *The Doctor* from Touchstone Home Video?

3:00 pm   *The Disney Afternoon.* Two hours of Disney cartoon entertainment. Plenty of yuks for grown-ups too.

5:00 pm   Go to The Disney Channel in search of youthful energy. It's *Kids Incorporated*, followed by the *Mickey Mouse Club.* M—I—C, see ya real soon...

6:00 pm   Syndicated rebroadcast of *Golden Girls.* Those gals are a hoot, and laughter is the best medicine.

6:30 pm   You've been watching too much TV! The soundtrack to *Beauty and the Beast* is an entertainment in itself (and platinum, too!). Eat something light and healthy.

7:30 pm   Feeling a lot better, aren't you? Chances are, there's a movie theater a few minutes away. Why not see that new Buena Vista release (consider it research). If you haven't quite recovered, then stay home and plan that vacation you've been putting off. The sun never sets on a Disney theme park, you know. Hmmm. Tokyo or Paris, central Florida, or maybe Anaheim. Remember all the employee discounts!

9:00 pm   A good contemporary film, a concert, an undiscovered gem, or a Hollywood classic. Turn The Disney Channel back on; it's *Disney Night Time.*

11:00 pm   Isn't it way past your bedtime? Don't you have to work tomorrow? Sweet dreams (Unplug the phone.)

The Walt Disney Company OVERVIEW booklet, branded with the Corporate Synergy logo, was a huge success with all the executives in our database, including top company management. We even received a note from Walt Disney Studios Chairman Jeffrey Katzenberg remarking how much he loved the piece and how he was going to carry it around in his pocket. He said it was a keeper. Lesson learned—sharing good information, with an added dash of creativity, opens communication pathways.

Another home run that generated awareness for the department was the production of a four-minute video synergy video. Linda Warren told me it was one of the projects she felt was one of her greatest successes for the company. It was called "It's Synergy", and through music and video clips entertainingly illustrated how singular projects spread exponentially through the company. The entire piece was scored using the original sound track from *The Little Mermaid's* Academy Award-winning song "Under the Sea", except that the lyrics were rewritten to a new song called "It's Synergy".

Putting the video together was a big and expensive undertaking. While a producer was put in place to ultimately cut picture to the music and lyrics, the first thing to do was actually produce the new "It's Synergy" song.

We drafted Harold Kleiner, a senior recording executive with Walt Disney Records, to oversee the production. We hired Samuel E. Wright, the original voice of Sebastian the Crab who provided the vocals to "Under the Sea", to record the new lyrics along with several backup singers.

Then Harold and I jetted off to the recording session in New York City. Wright brought energy and life to the new song, written by Eisner's chief speech writer Dan Wolf. See the lyrics below and sing along to the tune of "Under the Sea":

Spoken
Everbody listen to me
Disney is more than just Mickey Mouse
There's something else that separates
Them Disney folks from all the rest

Verse
The whole of the place is greater
Than the sum of its many parts
A world of collaborators
It's no place for a la carte

It's constantly so refreshing
As everyone interacts
The ideas they all are meshing
A land of the Panafax

Chorus
It's synergy
It's synergy
Before our own eyes
They cross-fertilize
At the place called Disney!

Most corporations stratify
All the folks love to alibi
At Disney, no shirkin'
Cast shares the workin'
It's synergy

Verse 2
It started they say, with Mickey
They loved his upbeat outlook
Movies, then toys, then quickly
Came records and picture books

Snow White and then *Fantasia*
You startin' to understand?
On TV, the ads amaze ya
I'm goin' to Disneyland!
Oh yeah!

Chorus 2
It's synergy
It's synergy
Ideas unfurlin'
Energy swirlin'
Somethin' to see

First there's a film with Ariel
Records, toys, clothes for stores to sell

Then there's more action
Theme park attraction
It's synergy!

Chorus 3
It's synergy
The word's convoluted
But so well-suited
It won't let us be

Holding meetings all the day
Invigorating interplay
We get the spirit
Love to be near it
It's synergy!

Bridge
There are robot machines
And toy figurines
CDs, magazines
And films on the screen
Cartoons evergreen
And theme parks pristine
Expansion overseas

The hotels are themed
The steamboats are steamed
Film financing schemed
New disney stores dreamed
All buildings they gleam
The work of a team
They're modern Medicis!

Spoken
That's right, man
You know what synergy really is?
It's when you take something that's really good
And you put it with something that's even better
Yo get something that's wonderful
You got it?
Good!

Chorus 4
It's synergy
It's synergy
When the turnstiles click all the while
It's music to me

With our teamwork we combust
Mix in a little pixie dust

Each team cast member
Jan. to December
It's synergy

Tag
Each Imagineer here
We are all peers here
It's synergy

Each Disney worker
Not one a shirker
All are creating
Interrelating
Constantly rappin'
To make it happen
With synergy!

Once the recording was complete it was handed over to a video producer who added appropriate clips in a slickly, quick-cut paced, four-minute video that told the Disney synergy story in a very entertaining way.

Segments included clips from *Beauty and the Beast* and then showcased product spin-offs from a variety of Disney businesses. Clips from the movie transitioned into the *Beauty and the Beast* live show at Disneyland, into Publishing's *Beauty and the Beast* storybooks, into Walt Disney Records *Beauty and the Beast* CDs, into Home Video's *Beauty and the Beast* DVDs, etc.

More examples of a variety of different cross-promoted projects were also incorporated, and by the end of a short four minutes, viewers of the video could actually "see" how synergy worked in Disney's vast entertainment empire. And, the best part, the video was regularly updated with old clips being easily replaced with new ones to always reflect the current synergy status of the company. The music stayed the same.

Linda remembered the first time she showed the video to Frank Wells: "I remember when Frank first saw it, he couldn't believe how great it was. He was just over the moon about it."

Warren had come up with the idea for the "It's Synergy" video because she knew it could be used in a variety of ways within the company, all of which would underscore Michael and Frank's synergy mission. She continued, "Most companies would never spend the time, the money, and the effort we put into that video. Produced with Walt Disney Records executives, lyrics written by Michael's speech writer, recording sessions done in New York with the movie's original tracks, bringing in Samuel E. Wright and backup singers to make it the best it could be."

"It's Synergy" became a useful, popular tool in our ever-growing synergy bag of tricks. It also inspired the still-in-production "Company Clips" reel that plays in *every* room/cabin at Disney resorts and on cruise ships.

CHAPTER TWENTY-TWO

Establishing a Synergy Committee

An internal marketing group representing key Disney business units had been established by Art Levitt before I arrived on the scene when Corporate Synergy and Special Projects was known as Corporate Marketing. It consisted of about 30 mid-management marketers who would gather together every quarter to discuss their current projects.

At that time, it was not so much a proactive activity as an informational session with each person given a few minutes to discuss their current and upcoming projects. It was an informative, but not very actionable assembly. To me, the meeting was more about each person "press-releasing" their accomplishments rather than working together to find ways to proactively plan ahead and discuss cross-promotional possibilities.

While having this type of meeting was a first step, the structure needed to be changed moving forward. All of us in Corporate Synergy were more interested in generating cross-promotional marketing results from such gatherings. I started from scratch to put together the people who needed to attend what became monthly synergy meetings. From the marketing database that had been created, and working with the VP of Synergy and the heads of each business unit, a "key" synergy contact for each division was selected. All were middle management (directors and VP level) that would represent their business unit on an ongoing basis and be designated as the synergy contact.

Importantly, the key contact never changed unless that person left the company or moved on to another position. This assured consistency of thought from every division, and established that individual as the go-to person in their business unit on all synergy matters. Our Synergy Committee ultimately consisted of 60 carefully selected marketing and/ or entertainment executives, one for every Disney business unit. At each of our meetings we were speaking to and interacting with the entire Walt

Disney Company.

The Corporate Synergy Committee members were chosen with two criteria in mind. First, they had to have enough title power to move the marketing ball forward within their own divisions, and secondly they also had to be creative, have an outgoing personality, and be open to new ideas. MBAs were not necessarily the target. We wanted an enthusiastic group. That's a key component if successful synergy was going to occur.

Corporate Synergy was to be the center hub, then each synergy contact served as a spoke in the wheel that would put the entire organization on a synergy roll. Keep in mind that this group was comprised of our mid-management "worker bees", while Eisner and Wells, along with the Synergy VP, were working in parallel at the most senior levels of the company. It was a two-prong approach.

Once the new Synergy Committee was put into place, a Synergy News memo went out to our entire database making all the players aware of the "first in line" in each business unit when it came to discussing new synergy ideas, offering synergy advice, answering questions about a given project within that division, and so forth.

Synergy committee members became point people representing their individual business units. Marketing and creative executives no longer had to try to figure out which way to turn within the vastness of the Disney empire when they had a question or a new concept to discuss. Start with the synergy person. Either they would help or, at the very least, point you in the right direction. In time, the committee members became recognized as the internal "go-to" people on divisional marketing matters.

We accelerated our synergy meetings to being held once a month instead of once a quarter. Being Disney, a monthly two-hour Synergy Committee meeting had to be more than just a meeting. In the beginning, we needed to use every enticement possible to make sure everyone showed up for the sessions. Our meetings were always scheduled for 9:00 am and almost always on a Friday to make it easier for those committee members who flew in each month from their more distant locations (mainly New York and Orlando-based business units).

Breakfast was always provided before the meeting. I'm not talking coffee and Danish, I'm talking a lavish spread of fruit, muffins, bagels, lox, croissants, rolls, cereals, coffee, tea, juices, and more. Not only did people show up, they arrived early to enjoy the spread and to chat with other members of the committee...a great relationship builder.

Another important factor was that all meetings had a set agenda, distributed to all committee members prior to the gathering, to keep everything on point. Synergy Committee members could request adding their particular marketing project on the agenda for group discussion. We always focused on the key company drivers in those meetings (usually stemming from the motion pictures and theme park divisions); however, all reps had an opportunity to seek synergistic partnerships on whatever might be a high priority in their own business unit. Everyone was heard.

Jane Gordon-Mazur, a Synergy Committee member representing Walt Disney Records, said, "I loved having the synergy role. It gave me a voice in the company for my division. I could bring so many things to the table from my own perspective and that was very important."

Much of Gordon-Mazur's cross-promotional strength was tied to the film division, since so many of the animated movies were musically based. "The music was such a big part of films like *Beauty and the Beast*, *Aladdin*, and *The Lion King*. Of course, we produced all the soundtracks and those songs were ultimately used in Disney Publishing's Sing-Along books, in-park at Disneyland and Walt Disney World, in stage shows, and in so many other ways that allowed us to cross-promote our individual product throughout the company. Plus, the synergy meetings were so important because we discussed plan-ahead activities so we were always in front of the opportunities, not behind them. The fact is, we all played a part. Sometimes it was bigger and sometimes it was smaller. You kind of had your turn."

Leading each meeting was Linda Warren, who was the closest person to the top of the synergy ladder, Michael Eisner. Her voice carried his corporate priorities to all branches of the Disney synergy tree. Those branches, in turn, related the information to their divisional constituents. Some members of the committee, representing Disney's larger business units such as theme parks, eventually created their own synergy committees within those divisions as well. The aim was to always have the right hand of marketing always know what the left hand of marketing was doing, throughout the organization. One individual for one business unit was the corporate formula.

Agenda items for each meeting usually consisted or five or six key topics, each presented by the committee member representing that business. Open discussion with the whole group followed and often led to new and mutually beneficial synergy opportunities. Follow-up then moved beyond the meeting walls for all interested parties to further explore on a one-on-one basis.

Another Synergy Committee member, Cindy Spodek, from Buena Vista Home Video International, remembered, "What was amazing about those meetings is that there was sixty or so people in this one room that were empowered to really make things happen at every level of the company. The business lesson I took from it was that it worked because Eisner and Wells led by example. They were the big power players that drove everything from the top. The fact is, I got my masters in Marketing at Disney."

Pumping up the synergy enthusiasm level among committee members even further, attendees often came armed with promotional items, one for every committee member, plugging a current venture within their division. All good marketers love to hand out swag, don't they? T-shirts, books, logoed baseball caps, buttons, cassettes (do you remember cassettes?), beach towels, and more became meeting take-a-ways. Promoting from within had its perks.

Sometimes, our meetings even held surprises for the attendees, whether with special guests (Michael Eisner, business unit presidents, or film directors, for example) or unusual presentations. I remember one meeting in particular that gave us all quite a start. As we all got settled in our seats for the meeting to begin, in walked three men, all wearing white and carrying aluminum trashcans and drumsticks. Setting the trashcans down, they started playing them, loudly and amazingly well. They entertained us with a rhythmic good time. Talk about a morning wake-up call.

The trio was the trashcan musicians who entertained guests at Disneyland every day. My Synergy VP thought it would be a great way to start our meeting off with a "bang", so she drafted them into service. What a treat and what a way to get our monthly gathering off to a roaring start. You never knew what to expect at a synergy meeting.

In 1992, three years into her tenure at the studio, Linda Warren, was summoned back to Walt Disney World where she accepted the position of senior vice president of Sales. She had accomplished a great deal in Corporate Synergy and set the stage for everything to come. Warren went on to became senior vice president of EPCOT, becoming the first woman to lead a Disney theme park and finally rising to head of marketing for Walt Disney World, following in the footsteps of her former boss, Tom Elrod. She climbed the Disney ladder and earned every step.

Replacing Linda and continuing to lead the charge in Corporate Synergy was Jody Dreyer, another long-time Disney World marketing executive. She became my new boss and the role fit her like a glove. Dreyer, like Warren, was very upbeat, motivational, and very smart. She spoke of her predecessor, saying, "Linda really built the synergy architecture at the company. She set a strong foundation that put me on the right path."

While 1992 was a big year for me, feeling my way as to how things were going to work with Linda gone and Jody on board, it was also a really big year for the company.

Euro Disney (now Disneyland Paris) opened on April 12, 1992, in Marne-la-Vallée, France, just outside of Paris. While I was not personally involved in this event, many of my Disney colleagues, and indeed some who were synergy team members, had been sent to Paris to work on the project. They were there for months, and in some cases took up residence for several years to work on-site bringing their marketing expertise to the launch of the new park. Needless to say, the Disney marketing machine was in full swing on this project, albeit more internationally focused.

In the meantime, Jody was settling in as the head cheerleader for Corporate Synergy. She was, as it turned out, passionate about it and lived it 24/7, as did I. We developed into a great team. And she loved her two bosses, Eisner and Wells, and described them as "wickedly smart". She set about following their lead by immediately diving into the synergy pool. Her first priority was building strong relationships across the company. She said, "To me, synergy was as much about developing strong ties across the company as was the information we were passing along. I always felt that synergy was more relational than transactional. Someone once took me to task on that, insisting that there does have to be the transaction, there has to be activity that does make it work, and I said, "Right, but you'll never get to that if you're not in relationships first."

Eisner felt the same way. "Michael treated it as relational. I can remember times when someone from Strategic Planning or Finance would come to an Eisner meeting and in talking about a specific project would say, "I can't figure out how to make this work on paper, or this isn't going to pencil out." Then Michael would say, "Well, we're going to do it anyway because it's the right thing to do and he knew we had the internal relationships to pull it off."

Dreyer explained those relationships as being akin to functioning in a big family rather than a diversified company, as in Eisner's well-attended Monday Lunch where each attendee was seated around a round conference table. "It was the world's biggest round table so no one could be in a back row or hide behind anyone. There was no cover and everyone was expected to participate."

Often, according to Dryer, when an important decision had to be made on a given synergy project, Eisner and Well purposefully chose opposite sides of the debate. "There wasn't any discussion where attendees could go either way. It was either they were on one side or the other. We always joked that Michael and Frank were kind of like the mom and dad of a big Italian family (and were jokingly called Mom and Dad by the group). After expressing their views they would go around the table to the "kids" and see what each of them had to say. Based on the responses, the pair could gauge which of the kids was going to cause problems, which was going to need to be disciplined, etc."

The discussions were always totally open, exposing real feelings and sometimes becoming quite heated. But again, Dreyer said, "It was like family and opening up to your brothers and sisters. It could be a free-for-all and nothing was sacred, but by being so, there was never a secret agenda in that room, it was all out in the open."

It was Dreyer's job to set the agenda for Michael's Monday Lunch and what synergy items were to be discussed: "That's how we pushed all synergy directives along and kept them moving on a positive path at the most senior levels of the company. I couldn't let anything fall through the cracks."

Another thing that never happened was that when discussing what each business unit was working on from a synergy perspective, no one could ever have nothing to report. "They couldn't just casually say something like, "oh, everything is good", no one could get away with that and they knew it. The meetings promoted action, every time."

It was also Dreyer's charge to follow-up on actionable items. "One of my biggest jobs was the follow-up. The people at the table were the top decision makers. If something was going to happen synergy-wise in a business, the person who was going to make the ultimate decision was there. If something came up at lunch in that a person wasn't playing the synergy game, my goal was to get them to play. Michael just assumed that I was going to get back to him if that was not happening. I was the queen of follow-up, making sure it did happen. An example might be with a giant company synergy project like *The Lion King*, when Eisner might say at the Monday Lunch, "What is everybody doing?" and start going around the table. Boy was there embarrassment if somebody said, "Well, my division doesn't have much to do with this." Michael was like, "yeah right", and say, "Jody will get back to you." Nobody got off the hook."

Dryer summed her job up quite well. "I viewed my position as a traffic controller for the company, like at an airport. I was making sure to maximize the synergy opportunities that emanated from all our business units."

She did so on a senior basis, keeping every project moving throughout the organization directly under the guidance of Michael Eisner and Frank Wells. I did so on a mid-management basis, primarily from a communications standpoint directly under Dreyer's guidance. Nothing was ever at a standstill. But Dreyer was also aware that she sometimes had to bring out those big, glow-in-the-dark yellow reflectors to ward off any possible train wrecks in our traffic management system. I don't think we ever had a collision.

There were times, however, that Corporate Synergy had to work especially hard to bring a potential synergy partner into the fold. Dreyer derived an immense sense of satisfaction when they were finally won over, and they always were. "There were just some people who were highly skeptical of the process and how it could benefit their division. Winning them over was one of my favorite parts of working in synergy. I always felt like, "I can make them see the advantages", and that actually energized me. Then once they had a synergy win, even a small one, it was like a light bulb went off and they became some of our best converts."

Sometimes obstacles did get in the way. "What could take the air out of a room were the people that wanted to financially quantify synergy. I hated that discussion. The money people could suck the life out of synergy before it happened. Fortunately, following that approach was not our priority, although it played its rightful role in the overall process."

Dreyer was more in step with her former Walt Disney World mentors, Tom Elrod, Phil Lengyel, and Charlie Ridgway who were "crazy promotions people" that would come up with outrageous ideas and then just do them. "I'm just more comfortable in that environment. We'll put order to the budget and figure out logistics, of course, but let's not start there."

Synergy also came into play for Disney marketing events and shows staged outside the confines of the studio and theme parks. Dave Goodman, then vice president of an internal entertainment group called the Walt Disney Special Events Company, was responsible for film premieres, the opening of Disney Stores, and any other marketing event that took place outside of the parks. He said, "My group put together over 1,800 Disney events annually that were presented in cities worldwide. They originated from every division in the company and I often relied on synergy to make my job work better. I started by going to the presidents of the parks (dependent on which park was expected to be impacted by a given event), then I'd speak to the head of Feature Animation and Walt Disney Imagineering, sometimes the head of Film Distribution. Depending upon the concept for what we were going to produce, it might include also going to the heads of Merchandising, the leaders of Foods, Operations, Security, Safety, Marketing, and the Hotels and Resorts."

Goodman would meet with all the appropriate executives before he started to actually move forward with a given scenario. "I'd explain the idea for what we were about to put together and which business unit was driving it, in what city or cities it was going to be presented, the timing, etc. Then, I'd ask how we could help them and at the same time maximize the effectiveness of the event by possibly adding a promotional mention, inserting a musical number, or whatever, from their business unit into the project on a cross-promotional basis. Synergy, if you will."

According to Goodman, bringing all the different groups into the process at the beginning gave them input and ownership of the project and the motivation to help make it succeed. Any ideas that business unit leaders might have with regard to showcasing something from their own divisions in his project was noted and Goodman did his best to make it happen. "A winning event for me was one that brought together a lot of good ideas from smart people all over the company. It was always tailored to be a win-win...the results had to be stellar because Eisner and Wells never expected anything less."

As Michael's Monday Lunch meetings progressed over the years, so did our mid-management monthly synergy meetings where we all learned more and more about marketing across The Walt Disney Company directly from the people who worked the job everyday. It made us all better, and smarter, marketers.

Ideas bounced around our monthly meeting rooms like a high-performance rubber ball. Cross-divisional brainstorming sessions were often separately scheduled, as well. The exchange of ideas and the give-and-take of making a synergy project work, often quite a process, was...dare I say it...magical.

CHAPTER TWENTY-THREE

Synergy Communications Expand

Corporate Synergy created a number of communications tactics, in print, on video, and even with a Synergy Online intranet way back in the mid 1990s (I like to think we were on the cutting edge with that one!).

In addition to distributing Synergy News Memos, some of our other communications included a monthly information piece called "Synergy This Month" that provided our database with what synergies were in process, by business unit. Therefore, not only did we plan ahead, but we also kept marketers informed of what was happening on a current basis. I decided to use some psychology to foster new synergies with this communication.

First, how was I going to get all the key contacts from each division to provide Corporate Synergy with details of their activities each month so I could create a Synergy This Month report? Essentially, I was burdening them with having to do work for us.

As mentioned before, no one reported to Corporate Synergy. To that end, I tried to make their task as easy as possible. Did they have to put together a formal report to me each month? No. Did they need to make it look good for me? No. All I asked was for a brief listing or paragraph on what was happening synergy-wise in their divisions. It could be typed, or even just be a quick handwritten note faxed to my office. Whatever made it really easy for them, not for me, is what was important.

Even at that, getting the information from around the company in the early stages of this communication could be like pulling teeth. However— and this is where the psychology to foster new synergies came in—the monthly report listed activities by business unit and was distributed to the entire synergy database, as well as those at the highest levels of the company, including Michael Eisner and all his senior executives. My theory was that business units reporting synergy activities would come to be viewed as involved and proactive, while those not listed were "missing in action".

Everyone knew the powers-that-be would see the monthly report, and before long, more and more divisions started providing me monthly information. Human nature dictates that in order to look good to the bosses vs. looking like a deadbeat, new ideas will suddenly be generated from every corner of the organization.

Another informational piece that was distributed on an annual basis was a list of important upcoming company dates. For an entertainment company like Disney, significant dates in the organization's history always provided an added angle to inspire new product and/or special events via the various company business units. Therefore, anniversaries such as Mickey's 60th, Disneyland's 35th, Donald's 50th, and others, were need-to-know dates for our constituents to be able to plan ahead. Working with the Walt Disney Archives, a "Significant Disney Dates" list was developed.

An example, covering the years 1995 to 1999, is shown below. It was distributed to our database a year out, and released via a synergy communication called "Synergy FYI":

> For your information, following is a list of significant Disney dates from 1995 to 1999 that may be useful in planning future marketing strategies for your business. This list was compiled by the Walt Disney Archives.
>
> **1995**
> 65th—*Pluto, The Chain Gang* (1930)
> 50th—*The Three Caballeros* (2/3/45)
> 40th—Disneyland (7/17/55)
> 40th—*Lady and the Tramp* (6/16/65)
> 40th—*The Mickey Mouse Club* (10/3/55)
> 25th—*The Aristocats* (12/24/70)
> 20th—Walt Disney World Village (3/22/75)
> 10th—*The Black Cauldron* (7/24/85)
>
> **1996**
> 95th—Walt Disney's birth (12/5/01)
> 50th—*Song of the South* (11/12/46)
> 30th—*Winnie the Pooh and the Honey Tree* (2/4/66)
> 25th—Walt Disney World (10/1/71)
> 10th—*The Great Mouse Detective* (7/2/86)
>
> **1997**
> 65th—Goofy, *Mickey's Revue* (1932)
> 60th—*Snow White and the Seven Dwarfs* (12/21/37)
> 60th—Donald's nephews (10/17/37)
> 60th—Daisy Duck (1/9/37)
> 50th—*Mickey and the Beanstalk* (9/27/47)
> 40th—*Zorro* (10/10/57)
> 30th—*The Jungle Book* (10/18/67)

20th—*The Rescuers* (6/22/77)
20th—*Pete's Dragon* (12/16/77)
15th—EPCOT Center (10/1/82)
10th—The Disney Store (3/28/87)
 5th—Disneyland Paris (4/5/82)

1998
70th—Mickey Mouse/Minnie Mouse (11/18/28)
60th—*Donald Duck* comic strip (2/7/38)
60th—*Ferdinand the Bull* (11/25/38)
50th—*Melody Time* (5/27/48)
25th—*Robin Hood* (11/8/73)
15th—The Disney Channel (4/18/83)
15th—Tokyo Disneyland (4/15/83)
10th—*Who Framed Roger Rabbit?* (6/21/88)
10th—*Oliver & Company* (11/18/88)

1999
65th—Donald Duck (6/9/34)
50th—*The Adventures of Ichabod and Mr. Toad* (10/5/49)
15th—Touchstone Pictures (3/9/84)
10th—Disney-MGM Studios (5/1/89)
10th—*Honey, I Shrunk the Kids* (6/23/89)
10th—*The Little Mermaid* (11/15/89)

A monthly Synergy Calendar was another of our communications. It was quite literally a single page per month printed calendar with boxes for each day of the upcoming month that listed company goings-on in the appropriate date boxes, often with overlapping events. Such listings included film openings, product releases, book releases, Disney tours, special events, TV specials, sports schedules, and more. Anyone could look at any given month and see significant day-to-day marketing and promotional happenings throughout the entire company in one glance. Everyone in our database received all synergy-branded communications. No one could say, "I didn't know about that."

Putting together the Synergy Calendar once again required asking for more effort from our key synergy contacts. But we were in the swing of things by the time this informational piece got off the ground and only a phone call from my assistant, Jesse Priore, was all that was required. Jesse got it from the horse's mouth and handled putting the data together on a monthly basis.

Again, we made extracting information as simple and easy as possible. In fact, we did as much as possible to give, give, give, not take, take, take; our constituents had just too much to do already, and we respected that.

Bi-annually we also compiled a list of need-to-know "Key Dates" across the company for our constituents. In the following example, the time period covered is May to December 1998 (for brevity, I've just included the months of May and June). It was our job to keep everyone on the same synergy page:

- May 19: ABC Fall prime-time announcement
- May 21: New Tomorrowland opens at Disneyland
- May 28–31: Corporate retreat at WDW
- June 5: Synergy meeting in LA
- June 5: Mulan premiere at the Hollywood Bowl
- June 7–10: Global synergy meeting in LA
- June 10: American Teacher Awards taping in LA
- June 16: Publishing synergy meeting NYC
- June 19: *Mulan* opens wide
- June 19: DisneyQuest opens at WDW
- June 19-28: Summer X-Games
- June 20: American Teacher Awards airs on The Disney Channel
- June 22–25: Synergy online boot camp in NYC (Disney NY entities)

It was also understood that while my department interacted with business units across the company, we were never to presume we knew more about their business than they did, because we didn't. That's why material used to compile most of our synergy documentation was unedited from the source. And that applied not only to what they said, but also how they said it. Changing just a single word from an overview that we would include in one of our synergy communications could represent a complete misrepresentation of what they were reporting. Therefore, I only made grammatical changes to submitted notes and never changed their words, thus avoiding mistakes.

CHAPTER TWENTY-FOUR

Planning Ahead

To make all of the previously discussed tactics work, advance planning must take place, often one to two years ahead of the projects in the synergy line of sight. No one can create an internal cross-promotion, such as creating a new consumer product, producing a television show, or publishing a new book to promote a given company priority, overnight. If advance planning doesn't take place, it probably won't happen and opportunities are lost.

To counter this challenge, we created a "Corporate Priorities List" on an annual basis focusing on key projects one to two years ahead of release. It was our synergy road map. For a major animated film, for example, at least two years might be required in the planning stages. A major theme park celebration needed twelve to eighteen months. The list was distributed not only to the Synergy Committee, but everyone in our synergy database.

The Corporate Priorities List was usually just a simple one-page document. The list took every business unit into account, not just those like the film division or the theme parks that often led the synergy train. The priorites for 1995 are shown below:

Walt Disney Company Priorities 1995

- *Pocahontas* animated film
- Disneyland's 40th Anniversary/Opening Indiana Jones Adventure
- *The Lion King* Home Video
- *Disney Encyclopedia of Baby and Child Care*
- Walt Disney World/Epcot '95/New Tomorrowland
- The American Teacher Awards
- *Gargoyles*
- The Disney Institute

Although we identified the company emphasis on an annual basis, the priority listed projects were not the only synergy ones we expected to be pursued. We merely outlined key activities to help our constituents plan ahead.

For many reasons, the positive effects of planning ahead for any business can ultimately be reflected in achieving higher overall corporate success.

By doing so, leaders and organizations better execute projects, reach their goals, and fulfill their vision. The Chinese philosopher Confucius said, "A man who does not plan long ahead will find trouble at his door." Very true.

And just how did we at Disney get ahead of the Corporate Priorities list in terms of planning ahead? For those that were of major significance, such as a new animated film like *Pocahontas* or the technology that brought the toys to life in Pixar's *Toy Story*, it required the full cooperation of the root business.

For example, for a major animated film, the timeline for getting the synergy wheels turning might look something like this:

Early planning started about 12 to 24 months prior to the opening of the film with a high-profile, invitation-only Feature Animation presentation to a gathering of worldwide Disney marketing, entertainment, and creative executives, along with Disney product licensees. Because it was such a large gathering, Disney often rented the National Academy of Television Arts and Sciences Theater located in North Hollywood to make the presentation.

The event was hosted by Disney Animation president Peter Schneider, along with senior Feature Animation executives, key animators, and the film's producer and director. Michael Eisner and Jeffrey Katzenberg often addressed the audience, as well.

During the several hour program, the audience was treated to sneak-peek preview screenings of early in-production clips, often in the pencil sketch stage. A special guest, such as singer/actress Lea Salonga who sang during the Feature Animation presentation on *Mulan*, also entertained them. The reasoning behind such a high-profile overall presentation was to generate early awareness of story, characters, style, music, voice talent, and so forth.

A secondary purpose of holding the early Animation program was to create "event film" excitement within the Disney organization and with licensees who need a long lead time to develop product lines. This annual presentation was always a standing room-only event.

As we moved to intermediate planning, perhaps 8–12 months prior to the film's release, project specific synergy meetings were held to discuss and brainstorm cross-promotional ideas for the film with key synergy representatives in every company business. Ongoing from a synergy standpoint, in-the-works cross-promotions were continually discussed and moved forward at monthly synergy meetings, both in large group sessions and smaller one-on-one dialogues.

To complement all, a variety of synergy communications were distributed to our database to provide marketing updates on the film to our nearly

1,000 Disney marketing, entertainment, and creative executives who were in the synergy loop. Information focused on internal cross-promotional activity to date.

Of course, while much communication was happening at the mid-management level under my watch, the push was also happening at Eisner's Monday Lunches with the heads of all the business units, and with follow-up by Jody Dreyer, Synergy Vice President. A final synergy plan, having begun nearly two years prior to the film's release, ultimately touched every corner of the company.

Another priority event that was planned well in advance that proved impressive from a synergy standpoint was when Walt Disney World held a three-day media event in early October 1992 focusing on the opening of their Splash Mountain attraction. In fact, synergy was so on view at that particular gathering that *Variety*, the trade bible of Hollywood, ran the following feature story on October 7, 1992, titled, "Disney Promotional Party Showcases Synergy", tossing in a bit of sarcasm along the way:

> Synergy has long been one of the most over-used terms in the entertainment industry, a sort of high-falutin' buzzword that means, in simple Schwarzenegger-type lingo: "Ve're big, and ve vill use our size to crush you."

> Those attending Disney's three-day media blitzkrieg in Orlando last weekend, however, witnessed an awesome display of synergy in its purest form, with various arms of the company all pumping into one huge orgy of promotion and hype.

> Thousands of media representatives showed up at the weekend events, which included the Disney World opening of Splash Mountain, work-in-progress screenings of *Aladdin*, groundbreaking on the Television Hall of Fame Plaza, and press events by both Walt Disney Corporate and Disney TV.

> There were television reporters from places like Memphis, Tampa, and Tallahassee shooting questions at Michael Eisner about Euro Disneyland and his status as a member of "the cultural elite"—reporters whose local viewers probably couldn't care less about the answer to either question.

> Nevertheless, all those reporters (and some of their bosses) were in Orlando, drawn by the lure of the many events, and as long as they were there they had to do something to justify the visit to their stations, or newspapers, or whatever.

> The whole weekend underscored how cleverly a company like Disney can use its multiple operations to feed other areas. That's why competitors such as Warner Bros., Paramount, Universal, and Sony have at least flirted with their own ventures to be equally diverse, from

Universal Studios to Sonyland to Six Flags.

By the same token, it also demonstrated why the entertainment industry has gradually concentrated into a handful of major players and why further consolidations, sans limiting regulation, is almost inevitable, leaving smaller companies with a choice: be on the inside looking out, or on the outside looking in.

One animated hit, Disney executives point out, feeds revenue into different arms of the company like a spider web, with strands extending into feature films, television, merchandising, licensing, home video, retail stores, costumed characters for theme parks, etc.

During the weekend, Disney exploited that diversity with a vengeance, as well as its status as one of the few legitimate brand names in the entertainment industry.

Granted, that emphasis on synergy can reach a teeth-gnashing saturation point, such as referring to all employees as "cast members", which brought to mind a joke about the circus janitor who didn't want to leave because it would mean getting out of show business. "Oh cast member, I dropped my Mickey fudgicle, can you sweep it up?"

Others might get a little queasy about reports that senior managers must each spend a day at the theme parks as a costumed character—actually a brilliant means of evoking a unity of feeling among employees as well as fun for outsiders, who can try and guess which character (Goofy? Chip?) best fits the exec.

Still, in the larger scheme of things, all of this builds toward synergy in the term's most important sense as those in showbiz use it: that the various parts, taken together, create a much bigger whole, and as such enjoy advantages within each individual area.

If a station manager wants to take his kids to Orlando, for example, that can help the public relations wing generate news coverage, or the syndication operation clear a show, or the marketing folks in seeking a movie tie-in.

Even cab drivers in Orlando talk with reverence about the Disney marketing machine, from the hardball they play with vendors to the savvy with which they've manipulated local officials. There's admiration, if not necessarily fondness, in most of their words.

Most of all, Disney's strategy and that of the other studios reflects the fact that the big will keep getting bigger because it makes sense for them to do so—one reason why rumors about eventual network-studio mergers won't go away.

What does that leave for the little guy? For those determined to remain independent, the answer, with apologies to Mickey, is to say a silent prayer and try to build a better mousetrap.

The mousetrap was indeed working like a well-oiled synergy machine in all Disney business units.

On the animated movie side of the business, under the leadership of Roy Disney and Jeffrey Katzenberg, the hits were piling up. Under their watch, huge successes included *The Little Mermaid, Beauty and the Beast,* and in 1993, *Aladdin.* These films were among the first that inspired massive synergy activity to percolate in every corner of The Walt Disney Company. In fact, in that year, Disney's Annual Report touted the merits of synergy to the stockholders with an overview of *Aladdin's* success:

> Nineteen-ninety-three was "The Year of Aladdin" for The Walt Disney Company...for millions of reasons.

> If *Aladdin* had only been the animated motion picture hit that it was, and nothing else, it would have been wildly successful. The film ultimately earned $218 million at the box office in the United States and $100 million through year-end internationally. But because one plus one often equals three at The Walt Disney Company, *Aladdin* became a great deal more than a hit movie.

> People didn't just want to see the movie. They wanted to read it, wear it, listen to it and play with it...and Disney's many operating units made those things happen. To meet this demand, Disney Consumer Products licensed a full line of books, apparel, recordings, and toys that, more than a year after the release of the movie, are still selling briskly. During 1993, *Aladdin* merchandise provided the largest percentage of the Disney Stores' total business. To date, more than 4,000 *Aladdin* products have been created worldwide.

> Subscribers to the Disney Channel got an insider's look at the film, thanks to a 30-minute special on the making of *Aladdin.* The Channel also broadcast segments that promoted the film between its regularly scheduled shows. KCAL, Disney's independent Los Angeles TV station, joined the *Aladdin* parade, producing its own special, *The Magic of Aladdin.*

> Soon after the movie came out, a new *Aladdin* parade was unveiled at the Disney-MGM Studios and at Disneyland. Then, in July, Aladdin's Oasis opened at Disneyland. This is a popular new restaurant and stage show in Adventureland themed after the movie. And, of course, *Aladdin* characters have become instant "stars" at Disney parks around the world.

> Original artwork from the film was auctioned by Sotheby's for more than $1.35 million. One single piece, depicting Aladdin and Jasmine on their magic carpet ride, brought $25,300. For the budget conscious, limited-edition serigraph images reproducing scenes from the film were sold at the Disney Stores, the parks, and through a network of Preferred Galleries.

In October, the *Aladdin* video game for Sega Genesis was released. This landmark event marked the first time that Disney was an active partner in the creation of a video game. Disney animators were directly involved in the design of the game, which was cited by *Time* magazine as a major step forward in interactive videos.

In the fall of 1994, *Aladdin* will return as the newest entry in *The Disney Afternoon*. Every weekday afternoon, "Aladdin" will be featured in a new half-hour television episode, along with Jasmine, Abu, the Magic Carpet, Iago, the Genie, and all the other stars from the film.

These are just some of the highlights of *Aladdin's* impact. There have been literally thousands of smaller ways that the film has created opportunities throughout the company, from *Aladdin* theme park window displays to *Aladdin* Halloween costumes to *Aladdin* giveaway toys at Burger King.

All of this synergistic interaction is possible because The Walt Disney Company continues to focus on entertainment, the common thread that weaves through all of Disney's far-flung enterprises. As a result, opportunities constantly arise in one area of the company that in turn ignite additional opportunities in other areas. This is why one plus one will continue to equal at least three as Disney maintains its leadership in worldwide entertainment.

CHAPTER TWENTY-FIVE

The Day the Music Died

Under the almost decade-long leadership of Eisner and Wells, The Walt Disney Company enjoyed explosive growth. It seemed everything the pair touched turned to gold and profits were soaring. It was 1984 and Disney was firing on all cylinders. Then the unthinkable happened. On April 3, 1994, Frank Wells was killed in a helicopter crash. The *Los Angeles Times* reported:

> Frank G. Wells, the president and chief operating officer of the Walt Disney Co. and a key part of one of the biggest turnarounds in American corporate history, was killed in a helicopter crash Sunday during a skiing expedition in the rugged Ruby Mountains in northeast Nevada.
>
> Wells, 62, and four others were aboard the helicopter when it went down in a remote mountainside known as Thorpe Creek Canyon, about five miles south of Lamoille, members of the search party said.
>
> The pilot, Dave Walton, and Beverly Johnson, of Los Angeles and Wyoming, also died in the crash. Johnson's husband, Mike Hoover, was injured. He and their ski guide were taken to a hospital, Elko County Sheriff Neil Harris said. The injured were in critical condition.
>
> Johnson and Hoover are award-winning documentary filmmakers, sources said. They had filmed the guerrilla war in Afghanistan and their work appeared often on CBS News. Both were avid climbers and made several films about the expeditions. Hoover's short documentary, *Up*, won an Academy Award in 1984.
>
> The group had been heli-skiing in mountains where expert skiers travel for powdery slopes untouched by other skiers, officials said. Wells, at 6' 4", was an accomplished mountaineer who had climbed the highest peak on every continent, and had reached the summit of each one—except Mt. Everest.
>
> Wells had gone to Lamoille with his son Kevin for an Easter ski vacation, said a representative of Ruby Mountain Heli-Ski, the helicopter company, but his son was not aboard the copter when it crashed about 4:30 pm local time.

Actor-director Clint Eastwood was on the weekend trip as well, but he had left to return to his Carmel home an hour before the crash that claimed the life of Wells, who was his good friend and former attorney, said Eastwood's agent, Leonard Hirshan of the William Morris Agency.

The death of Wells was expected to send shock waves through an industry where management stability is rare. Wells and Disney Chairman Michael D. Eisner had become the model of such stability: their 10-year reign is a rarity in a business with high and frequent executive turnover. "There are no words to express my shock and sense of loss," Eisner said in a statement late Sunday night. "Frank Wells has been the purest definition of a 'life force' I have ever known.

"His wisdom, his charm, his zest for experience and challenge...his naked and awesome intelligence...set him apart and beyond. The world has lost a great human being."

Wells, a California native, Rhodes scholar, and former entertainment lawyer, was often overshadowed by the high-profile Eisner, but nonetheless was considered critical to Disney's turnaround that started when the two were named in 1984 after a struggle for Disney that threatened to break up the venerable Burbank company.

Even before the revival of Disney's fortunes—the company's market value leaped from $2 billion to $22 billion between 1984 and late 1992—Wells had a long history in the movie industry, including more than a decade at Warner Bros., where he began in 1966 as a vice president. He served as vice president and chairman of that company before he left in 1984 to join Disney.

The partnership served both Wells and Disney well. In 1990, Wells was the highest-salaried Californian, with total compensation from salary bonus and stock options of nearly $51 million.

Wells was also known as a bold mountain climber, who in 1981 set himself the goal of climbing the highest mountain on each of the globe's seven continents. He took a leave from Warner Bros. to co-author a book about the experience, *Seven Summits*.

As an undergraduate at Pomona College, which he attended with Roy Disney, Walt Disney's nephew, he had fantasized about being the first to conquer Everest—until a fraternity brother told him one day in 1953, "Well, we blew it. Some guy named Hillary just climbed it."

As a Rhodes scholar at Oxford University, he and a friend bought a private plane over one spring vacation to fly to South Africa and back. They only got as far as a crash landing in East Africa.

For all his button-down resume, Wells had an adventuresome spirit. The son of a Navy officer who spent much of his childhood living on Navy bases, he played championship high school football in Coronado, and in college played basketball and water polo.

A Stanford University law school graduate, Wells had been a partner in the Hollywood law firm of Gang, Tyre & Brown, which specializes in entertainment industry law.

In recent years, Wells had also earned a reputation as a behind-the-scenes mover in the effort to enact forestry protection legislation in northern California, backing a legislative effort that he termed "critical".

Wells' stewardship at Disney began in 1984. In a coup eventually led by Wells' former classmate, Roy Disney, the company's regime was ousted, and Eisner and Wells were brought in to salvage the operation.

To many at Disney, the day Frank Wells passed away is often described as the day the music died. Eisner and Wells had developed a very close working relationship, each balancing and complementing the other. Eisner said, "Frank was so rare. We had trust. If you look at the difference between him and others, I could say anything to Frank about the way I felt. I knew that if we were going to get in trouble, we were going to be in trouble together. I wasn't going to take the rap, and he wasn't going to take the rap. We would take the rap together."

Then, just three months after Wells' death, in July 1994, Michael Eisner underwent emergency quadruple-bypass heart surgery. Fortunately, he recovered quickly, but the loss of Wells had forced Eisner to re-think the executive roster at the highest levels of the studio.

Jeffrey Katzenberg, the studio chief, had hoped to replace Frank Wells as president of Disney, but Eisner did not think he was right for the job. After much infighting, including Katzenberg bringing a multi-million-dollar lawsuit against Disney (a story that was covered daily in the media), Katzenberg left Disney to form DreamWorks, SKG with Steven Spielberg and David Geffen, today an extremely successful enterprise. Joe Roth, former chairman at 20th Century Fox, was brought in to replace Katzenberg as studio chief.

A year later, Eisner hired Michael Ovitz, a good friend and then head of Creative Artists Associates (CAA), to fill Wells' role. Ovitz was one of the most high profile, successful entertainment executives in Hollywood at the time, with a celebrity roster a mile long. But within weeks of his arrival at Disney, it was clear that he did not fit into the Disney culture—at all. It was like trying to fit a square peg into a round hole. Fourteen months later, Ovitz was gone.

As was explained in Eisner's book, *Working Together*, in the years following Wells' death, Disney continued to grow, but it was different. "The company was never the same without Frank. I was never able to find another partner quite like him. Frank Wells and I had ten great years together. I had smoothed the way for him to be successful, just as he had smoothed the way for me. We strategized about how to keep our executives happy and our critics at bay. The years I worked with him were markedly different from the years I did not have Frank Wells as a partner."

Tony Baxter, former senior vice president of Creative Development at Walt Disney Imagineering, said, "Aside from the chance of working with Walt Disney himself, those first ten years of Michael and Frank as a team were the best that the company ever enjoyed up until that time. I think they really appreciated creative thinkers and often in large corporations senior-level managers don't really understand that process, but they did."

That was very important to Baxter, who was responsible for leading teams that created such popular Disney attractions as Big Thunder Mountain Railroad, Splash Mountain, Indiana Jones Adventure, Star Tours, and the overall design of Disneyland Paris, among other projects.

Baxter worked closely with the twosome on several high-profile Disney attractions and not only thought of them as colleagues, but also as friends. "I watched them work and Michael was a fountain of hundreds of unfiltered ideas. Sometimes the concepts were so crazy that you thought they were a joke, but you really didn't know. You couldn't afford to assume he was joking, as he sometimes did. We'd actually put time in on some of those ideas and then he'd say, "Why are you working on that, I was just kidding." Wells, on the other hand, would go through that fountain and could reach in and grab the jewels."

Baxter also remembered how much Wells loved Disneyland, wanting to keep abreast of everything, even down to what was on the park's menus. "I once saw Frank and his wife, Luanne, who had come to Disneyland unannounced, sitting at a table at one of park's restaurants. They had one of everything from the menu on the table. I went over to say hello and asked what they were doing there. Frank said, "We like to come down every so often and order everything on one of the menus because I want to be in touch. If someone asks me a question about the food in that restaurant I want to be able to tell them about it first hand."

After Wells passed away, Eisner was never the same. While his ideas kept coming, no one was ever as straightforward with him about those that were viable and those that were not. Baxter said, "Frank would literally tell Michael when he thought an idea was awful and Michael would listen and say, "Okay fine." No one seemed able to do that after Frank."

Walt Disney World marketing executive Phil Lengyel, who had a special bond with Wells, countered the public image of Wells as a "very corporate" executive. "He was far more human than people gave him credit for. His son and my daughter were both insulin dependent at very young ages. I would get phone calls from him at all hours of the day and night that had nothing to do with Disney, but had everything to do with modern Type

I diabetes research. He would say, "I just found this out or they're doing this at Stanford or this at the University of Massachusetts." When I got the call that he had been killed in a helicopter crash, for me, it was the day the music died."

But as with all great losses, life must go on, and so it did at The Walt Disney Company, albeit no longer with the same energy, business acumen, and passion of one of its most highly respected leaders.

CHAPTER TWENTY-SIX

Experiential Motivation

*Motivation is the art of getting people to do what you
want them to do because they want to do it.*

— Dwight D. Eisenhower

When you break down barriers, misunderstandings, prejudices, insecurities, divisions, territories, and hierarchies—you build teams. Get a group of people in a room having fun juggling balls or spinning plates, and barriers come down. Teams unite and work together when they identify a common purpose. Competition in teams or groups creates teams and ignites team effort. This concept was essential to keeping our Disney synergy team strong.

Early on in the process I realized the value of breaking down barriers and quickly put it to work to build our Disney synergy team by inviting the members of our first Synergy Committee to a bowling party. We were very lucky in that a private, 1950s-inspired, four-lane bowling alley exists at one of the buildings that comprise the headquarters of Walt Disney Imagineering headquarters in Glendale, California (that particular structure had once been a bowling alley and the Imagineers saved a few lanes—the retro-looking exterior was used as the locale of Jack Rabbit Slim's in the film *Pulp Fiction*).

The intimate bowling lanes were dubbed "Alleys in Wonderland". Most of our marketing executives either had no idea that such a Disney bowling alley existed or had heard about it, but never seen it. Therefore, just holding the group get-together at such an "insider" spot was an enticement to attend. Doesn't everyone love exclusivity?

I started the ball rolling (pardon the pun!) by getting the shirt sizes of each member of the Synergy Committee and not telling them why I needed the information, just that it would be a synergy surprise. We then had authentic bowling shirts made with a synergy logo knocking down bowling pins on the back and each of their names embroidered on the front. Of course, we sent out specially made invitations to the group, too.

RSVPs quickly arrived and everyone said "yes". The shirts were handed out at "Alleys in Wonderland" and everyone immediately put them on (over their shirts or blouses). Bowling food—pizza, nachos, desserts, beer, and sodas—was served buffet style. Importantly, teams were selected at random by picking names out of a hat. Mixing it up was the best way to build a new camaraderie. And we made it a real competition, promising the winning team a special surprise.

The evening was a great success on the fun scale. But more significantly new connections had been made, paving the way for synergistic partnerships to come. And we did have a winning team that was awarded "The 1st Synergy Bowling Tournament" trophy. Yes, we had trophies made, too. The bowling party is a good example of having fun together and building a team, but there was still much to be done on an experiential and motivational level when it came down to working synergy.

Corporate Synergy generated a "hands-on" approach in a variety of ways that were designed to light new synergy sparks. One such path consisted of multi-day meetings that we called a Synergy Familiarization trip or gathering. It was kind of like a mini-Disney Dimensions, the senior level synergy boot camp that lasted eight or nine days. Synergy Fams (as they came to be called) were usually three or four days of intense meetings, hands-on experiences, and in-person relationship building. Only Synergy Committee members were invited, and it was their division's responsibility to pick up the tab for their business unit representative's venture, since it often involved a trip out of town to another Disney location.

In 1996, our Synergy Fams, and in fact our entire synergy function, was elevated to a new level when an enormous new business unit was added to The Walt Disney Company. At a cost of $19 billion, Disney acquired Cap Cities/ABC, essentially doubling the size of the company. I worried that incorporating this powerful new asset into the synergy mix was going to a big challenge.

The Disney culture is very unique. You can feel it when you work anywhere in what is an immensely complex organization that is first and foremost an entertainment company. What permeates the organization is quality, employing the highest work ethics, exceeding expectations, and delivering unmatched service. Its cast members, Imagineers, and employees are committed, often passionate, about how they exemplify and contribute to those tenets, established by Walt Disney and reinforced to this day by all his successors. It is a palpable mindset.

In the most positive sense, integrating Cap Cities/ABC with Disney offered numerous new synergy opportunities. We now had the ABC Television Network, the ABC Internet Group, ABC-owned TV stations, ABC

Radio, ESPN, ABC Sports, Lifetime TV, Fairchild and Chilton Publications, and all the marketing forces behind those entities, on our roster. Could we make it work? Michael Eisner once again stepped in to set the expectations via the following ABC Welcome Letter that he sent to all ABC/Cap Cities executives:

> On behalf of The Walt Disney Company, I'd like to welcome everyone at Cap Cities/ABC to our newly consolidated corporation. The success, strength, and diversity we now share as one company is without peer in the entertainment industry.
>
> Among the many factors which we feel has contributed greatly to Disney's success is the ability of the company's many business units to cross-promote, or synergize, to elevate a given project to greater heights than it might ever have singularly achieved. A good example is the Disney animated film *Beauty and the Beast.* Beyond its run on the screen (Buena Vista Pictures), the project took on new energy as the characters came to life at the theme parks (Attractions), followed by the video release (Disney Home Video), then the Broadway show (Disney Theatrical Productions), Cast Album (Walt Disney Records), touring shows around the world, children's TV show (Buena Vista Television), and merchandise (Consumer Products, the Disney Store), among, many, many other cross-promotions.
>
> The synergy component is key to the success of The Walt Disney Company. With the addition of Cap Cities/ABC and all its divergent businesses to our roster, the opportunity for overall company cross-promotion is tremendous. I look forward to a future filled with unparalleled success; a ride that truly promises to be an "E" ticket.
>
> Michael D. Eisner

In turn, I sent out a Synergy News Memo to the Disney synergy database so as to familiarize them with the newly merged company by providing a historical overview of Cap Cities/ABC. I prefaced the history section by writing:

> As we welcome Cap Cities/ABC to the Disney family, it is important that we understand and appreciate their business structure and distinguished broadcast history to successfully move forward together. Interestingly, The Walt Disney Company actually forged a key alliance with ABC over forty years ago when Walt Disney needed additional financing to complete the building of Disneyland.
>
> ABC provided the needed funds in return for Walt providing the network with quality TV programming. It was from that agreement that the *Disneyland* show and the *Mickey Mouse Club* was born. In appreciation of the network's role in enabling Walt to complete the park, he honored ABC with four "windows on Main Street" above the

Candy Palace at Disneyland. A photo is attached of the fictionalized ABC windows that remain to this day. They read: ABC, ABC Typing, Acme Business College, and ABC Shorthand.

The ABC folks quickly understood that jumping into the synergy fray was the way to go, albeit a bit reticent to dive in with both feet at first. But in time, they did indeed get into the process, with a wonderful key Cap Cities/ABC synergy contact named Nancy DiBernardo appointed and added to our growing Synergy Committee.

Nancy flew in to Los Angeles every month to attend our synergy meetings and soon became one of us. She went on to maintain her own synergy constituency at ABC that she interfaced with on a regular basis carrying forth Corporate Synergy's messaging. She was the trunk of the ABC/CapCities synergy tree that spread the cross-divisional word through every branch of her company. And she did a great job of it. From a big picture perspective, ABC ultimately became a major synergy player supporting so many Disney priority projects with TV specials, TV series, talent support, and so much more.

With ABC on board, adding their slate of prime-time television series to our cross-promotional process prompted us to come up with a creative idea to get our synergy partners interested in promoting the network's new series entries. Synergy can be more difficult to inspire when it comes to TV series since no one is ever sure that the lineup of shows will be successful. They may only end up being aired for a few weeks and that can mean monies lost for supporting divisions. But, exposing long-time Disney business units to the new kid on the block was important. What we did was create a 1950s-themed "ABC Prime-Time Series Sneak Preview" meeting.

Synergy committee members were invited via a specially designed invitation that mirrored a newsstand *TV Guide*. To add to our themed event, we removed any chairs or tables in the meeting room and rented couches and recliners for relaxing and watching TV and old-fashioned TV trays for the pizzas we were serving for the late-in-the-day session. Everybody came!

The appropriate Cap Cities/ABC synergy team members were also always onboard for what became bi-annual Synergy Fam trips. One such venture was specifically held to welcome ABC executives to Disney and give them a taste of synergy up close and personal. The three-day gathering was the first ABC Synergy Familiarization trip to corporate headquarters in Burbank.

We had about 30 total invitees in total including ABC/CapCities synergy director, the VP of Program Planning and Scheduling, the VP and general manager of the television network, the director of TV Network Synergy, the VP of Media and Artist Relations, the president of Broadcasting, the manager of Children's Programming, the VP of ABC Marketing Research, the senior VP of ESPN Communications and HR, and Program and Marketing directors of ABC-owned stations.

We also invited members of our New York synergy team from Disney Publishing as well as the Walt Disney World Synergy director and members of her synergy team. It was a great opportunity for everyone to get to know each other. Corporate Synergy planned a jam-packed three days structured with both business and fun activities.

Our key focus of the sessions was to not only provide an overview of The Walt Disney Company and its businesses, but more importantly, to enable each of our guests to interact with many of the organization's key executives. They would also have the opportunity to meet the synergy groups mentioned above along with all members of the Burbank-based Synergy Committee. Several members of my staff and I attended throughout to lead the group and to make sure all went smoothly as planned.

Day one began with a welcome breakfast with members of the studio-based Synergy Committee and hosted by the Disney VP of Corporate Synergy and Disney's executive VP and chief of Corporate Operations. Following the welcome and morning meal, an overview of The Walt Disney Company was presented followed by presentations and discussions from top management from several key business units—Motion Pictures, Consumer Products, Disney Interactive, Home Video, the Disney Store, Corporate Alliances, and Brand Management. Following was a walking tour of the studio and then lunch at Feature Animation.

The VP of Communications for Feature Animation escorted the group on a tour of the Animation facility that is, of course, the heart and soul of The Walt Disney Company. Next, the group gathered in the Feature Animation Theater for a sneak peek and update on Disney's then upcoming next feature animation film release.

Following the movie they were addressed by the president of Feature Animation who presented an update on future projects and discussed the upcoming theatrical stage version of *The Lion King* on Broadway. Q&A followed.

Dinner was held at a local restaurant before getting everyone on a special Disney shuttle bus back to his or her hotel for the evening. They needed the rest. Day two would be equally busy.

Next morning everyone had to be packed (for a move to Anaheim later that day) and ready to be picked up by shuttle at 8:45 a.m. to be whisked off to Walt Disney Imagineering (WDI) in Glendale. This is the Disney arm that serves as the company's creative think tank and is charged with the responsibility of developing all Disney theme parks along with their rides and attractions. Most definitely a fun setting filled with wild and crazy creative geniuses.

Upon arrival, the group was met by the VP of Creative Development

Administration who introduced them to the vice chairman and principal creative executive of WDI along with WDI's president who presented an overview of their division. That session was followed by an update of ABC's involvement at the Disney-MGM Studios and an update of Disney's Animal Kingdom, the company's newest park that had not yet opened.

Shuttling once again, this time over to WDI's research and development (R&D) area for lunch, followed by a meeting with the executive vice president of Creative Technology and R&D who provided an overview of the facility. Then back on the bus to head 35 miles south to Anaheim and check in at the Disneyland Hotel, a bit of time for freshening up, and then on to Disneyland.

Met by the Disneyland Synergy Director, they were taken on a walking tour down Main Street, U.S.A. (who pointed the four ABC windows on Main Street), and then on to Adventureland for a ride on the park's newest thrill attraction, Indiana Jones Adventure. After surviving the ride and getting their bearings, it was off to a ghostly greeting at the Haunted Mansion where the group was trick-and-treated to a "spirited" dinner banquet. This one was an amazing first for Disneyland, hosting an elaborate themed dinner party actually inside an attraction.

Upon entering the antebellum Haunted Mansion (set in the park's New Orleans Square), we were served fine wine and elegant hors d'oeuvres as a pre-dinner start.

Soon we were escorted into a chamber with "No windows and no doors"— the Stretching Room—and the true start of the attraction experience. When we stepped out, dinner awaited us in the hallway where guests typically board their Doom Buggies.

A long banquet table (to accommodate over twenty people) was set within the hallway. Decorations featuring bats, goblins, cobwebs, candle -lit candelabras, and vases filled with dead flowers decorated the table. The menu was also themed to the attraction as was a wicked dessert drenched in blood (strawberry sauce). It was a delicious and amazingly creative repast that drew kudos from all. And of course there was only one way to exit our dinner location—we rode the attraction.

After their once-in-a-lifetime dinner experience, a current Disney film was screened at the Main Street Opera House in Town Square on Main Street, U.S.A. It was the end of a truly remarkable day that, as a commercial slogan once exclaimed, "It could only happen at Disneyland!"

Day three, energized and checked-out with bags packed and stowed away on the shuttle, our Fam guests enjoyed a Disney character breakfast at the Disneyland Hotel. A presentation on an in-development Disney regional entertainment venue came next, followed by a group cross-promotional brainstorming session on the new concept.

Lunch followed at Disneyland's very elegant and very private membership-only restaurant, Club 33. Joining the group for lunch was Disneyland's president, the SVP of Marketing and the VP of Marketing. After a great meal, our group had an hour's free time in the park before being dazzled by a presentation on an in-development new Disneyland parade by the director of Creative Development for Disneyland Entertainment.

Then it was time to get on board a shuttle bus for a short drive to Anaheim Stadium that served as the home base for Disney Sport's Anaheim Angels baseball team for a tour and overview of the arena with the director of Stadium Operations (Disney had purchased the Anaheim Angels in 1997).

A short hop to the Pond, the home stadium of the Mighty Ducks hockey team just down the road from Anaheim Stadium, came next. Dinner was served in the Pond's Executive Board Room with a visit from the president of Anaheim Sports, Inc. Everyone was then escorted to Disney's suite in the arena, stocked with an elaborate spread of drinks, finger foods, and munchies, to watch the home team hit the ice for a regularly scheduled game.

At about 8:45 pm, it was time to head for the exits and have our East Coasters board the Disney shuttle bus for transportation to John Wayne (Orange County) Airport where they boarded their magic carpet, the Disney corporate jet, for their trip back to New York.

The rest of the invitees were shuttled back to Burbank or Los Angeles International Airport to head back home. My staff and I had hopefully created a three-day motivating participatory event that would generate new and creative cross promotions, particularly from our new ABC partners, now members of the Disney synergy family.

Individual business units also hosted Synergy Familiarizations from their home bases once or twice a year. Of course, they too rolled out the red carpet for the invitees and treated all as VIPs in every way.

This is the way to make friends and influence people, especially those with whom you wish to forge great working relationships. We were, of course, very fortunate to be part of a company that understood that the cost of doing synergy business was worth the value ultimately derived.

Bottom line, like the amazing entertainment company we were, Disney synergists always put on a good show. It was in our DNA. Most importantly, it was also in Michael Eisner and Frank Well's DNA, and they enabled us to run with it. As Jody Dreyer so aptly put it, "They made it known from day one that we were all in it together."

CHAPTER TWENTY-SEVEN

The Synergy Landscape at Walt Disney World Resort

"With your little synergy department you had to move mountains," Laura Simpson, a nearly twenty-year Walt Disney World synergy executive once said to me. Referring to herself, she added, "And so did I."

Simpson, who served as Synergy director for the Orlando-based resort, was charged with establishing a huge synergy process that was incorporated across a property that covers over 27,000 acres and houses over twenty-five themed resort hotels, multiple golf courses, and four major theme parks: Magic Kingdom, EPCOT, Disney-MGM Studios (now Disney's Hollywood Studios), and Disney's Animal Kingdom. It was quite a task and she had to use great ingenuity to make it work. She did a great job while always remembering wise words of advice once given to her about synergy from Linda Warren. Simpson recalled that advice: "One of the most important things I ever learned came from Linda who told me never to use Michael Eisner's name to sell a synergy program. The program had to sell the program on its own merit."

It took Simpson a lot of influence and persuasion to fashion a win-win for both sides of the cross-promotional synergy equation. Plus, like myself in Corporate Synergy, budget-wise no other division supported the synergy function, so the enthusiasm for a given project had to be generated to make the deal. She recalled, "My game when dealing with Walt Disney World executives regarding cross-promotion was, "Let me tell you what's in it for you", which frankly is the thing everyone wants to hear."

Working synergy started as a slow process for Simpson who needed to get all her theme park divisions involved. She remembered the reaction when the computer animated film *Toy Story* became a priority, well in advance of the film release. "There was a lot of excitement coming from the studio because it was the first film from Pixar and everybody was told how big it was going to be. But nobody at Walt Disney World believed them. They were not always interested in what was going on in California. They were only concerned about what was happening in Orlando. But nevertheless, four *Toy Story* parade floats were designed although not built at that time."

Simpson also hit a brick wall when it came to developing *Toy Story* character costumes for in-park appearances by the film's toy stars. "Character costumes were designed, but they languished on the drawing board because the Entertainment division, which handled the project, did not want to pay to have them made. I had to take the money out of my meager synergy budget to get it done."

When the fabricated costumes were completed, they did not arrive at the Entertainment division, but rather at Simpson's office door. To add insult to injury, for two years Simpson had to pay for every time they had to be cleaned. But when *Toy Story* opened to phenomenal reviews and over-the-top success, Simpson's in-park constituents began to sing a different tune, eager to support what was then a huge Disney hit. "The parade floats were quickly built and I no longer had to pay any costs associated with the character costumes."

As with all company business units, with every cross-promotional "win" the synergy wheels turned a little easier.

But there were barriers to synergy, too. Finance issues, in particular, such as those experienced by Simpson in the *Toy Story* case, could sometimes be a difficult hurdle to advancing the process.

Attitudes, inability to act, and lack of timely information could also be formidable stumbling blocks. But Disney synergists were never ones to turn away from a challenge. More often than not, by hook or by crook, problems were resolved openly and in concert with all sides. Simpson said, "If there were barriers to synergy, most of the time we just jumped over them. We were driven to reach our goals through creativity, not just by the bottom line."

Spreading synergy across the vast Walt Disney World landscape led Simpson to develop her own methodology for getting the word out. "The way I would do it is that I would put together a synergy summit meeting back at Walt Disney World and I would invite all the key stakeholders in all the appropriate divisions based in Florida."

Simpson would then invite the division that headed a particular project (like the studio for a film release) to come in and do a presentation. Timing wise, this would happen perhaps a month after the project had been discussed at the monthly synergy meeting in Burbank that Simpson always attended. "Then we'd do a brainstorming session with everyone and ask them what they wanted to do to support the primary project. I always tried to make my group feel like it was their ideas that rose to the top because then they'd run with it. Importantly, ideas could never be pushed on a division, otherwise they'd never take ownership of it. Finance wise, they would budget against whatever ideas were realized through their own budgets."

Sometimes it was Simpson driving a Walt Disney World project for other business units to support. "It was then I had to work synergy from the other side. That's when I would knock on our partners' doors throughout the company to get them to synergize with us instead of the other way around."

Synergy Fam trips to Disney World were another aspect of the synergy process that Simpson handled with great finesse. Hosting the Synergy Committee crew, setting meeting agendas with key drivers of Disney World's high priority projects such as new attraction openings, anniversary celebrations, hotel openings, and special events; putting together special dining experiences; organizing tours; showcasing the resorts; and planning a welcome party were all aspects of a Synergy Fam that needed to be created, organized, and facilitated. Simpson recalled, "One of my favorite Synergy Fams in Orlando was the one we organized to showcase what we were doing for the millennium in the year 2000, a year ahead of the celebration. That was going to be our big theme and we were seeking synergy support from all around the company. I remember calling in my key Walt Disney World partners in the various divisions of the parks and I said, "I need to recreate what's it's going to look like in the parks in the millennium including the millennium parade and all this stuff you've described on paper. I need to bring it to life a year early." They thought I was a crazy person."

But Simpson knew that if she got to the creative folks and those that were really engaged in synergy from past experiences, they could make anything work. "What we ultimately did was create the whole millennium experience inside EPCOT's Energy Pavilion that we took over for the visiting synergy group. I had little money in my budget to pull these things off so what I would tell everybody to whom I had to sell the idea was, "Listen, you can all come and try out your creative concepts in what is really a kind of soft opening for what we're going to present when we do the real thing.""

She further encouraged those to be involved in putting together a welcome party. "The point of the welcome party was to try things that you've never done before. Make food that you've never made, things like that. Then if the party is really successful, you can have a photographer take photos that you can use to sell to Convention Services to use on other companies that come to us for a paid party."

Using only a small budget, but a great deal of ingenuity and imagination,

Simpson always put together great events and parties for the Corporate Synergy Fams to Walt Disney World. The best part was that afterwards the different divisions within the parks that were showcased would make back the money they spent tenfold by selling what they had done to other partners. Simpson said, "I'd always underscore to them that it was the smart thing to do. Having had all the executives from all the different divisions of the company attending gave all our people a super opportunity to showcase what they did to virtually the whole company."

Special niceties were always provided to the synergy group on such trips, as well. Upon arrival in our hotel room, we each received a welcome basket of goodies—fruit, cookies, chocolates, and wine—to snack on. Every basket contained a personally written welcome note from Simpson.

Checking in for the night, we'd find milk and cookies set by our bedside or perhaps a plate of hand-dipped, chocolate-covered strawberries. We were treated royally. But the goodies didn't end there.

After three or four days, we always left the property with a gift bag filled with items that promoted different aspects of Walt Disney World. I remember receiving such takeaways as a plush Disney World bathrobe, an Animal Kingdom briefcase, Disney World sweatshirts and T-shirts, Disney World cookbooks, and variety of fun items.

Greasing the synergy wheels was always appreciated, and as Simpson said, "Swag went a long way." The baskets, the gifts, the chocolate-covered strawberries were fun icing on the synergy cake. But the real joy was in what we actually accomplished with our business unit partners who often became good friends. Simpson explained, echoing the words of Jody Dreyer when she spoke of Eisner and Wells' senior-level executives meeting every week as family: "We were like a family. We worked together, we traveled together on the Fam trips, we bonded together. There was nothing like it. When you had that kind of strong family-like relationship with them, you didn't say "no" when they needed assistance with their programs, you always said "of course, how can I help you?" and figured out how to make it a win-win for both sides. Money can't buy these kinds of relationships; they must build naturally, and at Disney Synergy they did."

The win-win situation wasn't always 50/50 among synergy partners; there was a lot of give-and-take and one-hand-washes-the-other going on, too. "It might be that one time it was a 90/10 type of split, but that was okay because it was like, "Okay, we'll make it work even though we're getting the short end of the stick this time because next time I may get the lion's share." It always evened out. When it came to marketing, synergy was the "Disney difference".

Simpson credited Eisner and Wells with the synergy success achieved throughout the company. "Synergy to me was people that didn't just work in their silos anymore. Every one of them knew that their business had a bottom-line profit. And they all had goals they had to meet. Synergy was cutting across all those silos and all those divisions and figuring out a way to create win-win programs to make the company unbelievably successful. What was amazing to me was that it really only happened because Michael and Frank knew it was the right thing to do."

After 19 years working Disney internal cross-promotions, Simpson's synergy methodologies were ultimately working so well that if anything, her problem became having too many synergy opportunities from which to choose.

The thriving relationships that she had cemented over the course of her career still live on today, even after being retired for a few years. "There's not a week that goes by that I don't have a breakfast or lunch with a synergy partner from back then whether they're based here in Orlando or visiting from the West or East Coast."

In tribute to those close relationships, when Simpson retired she was not only given a party from her Walt Disney World friends and partners, but a second party took place in Los Angeles so that all her Burbank-based synergy partners could wish her well, too. That is a career well lived.

CHAPTER TWENTY-EIGHT

Synergy Goes High-Tech

One of Corporate Synergy's biggest steps forward was using what was then a relatively new technology—the internet—to internally foster synergy. We did so by creating a synergy intranet targeted only to our internal database to exchange marketing news and information. This was in the mid-1990s when company intranets were virtually nonexistent. But I got the approval to create an internal synergy website and to hire a webmaster to build it.

To keep our internal communications private, the completed intranet was password protected and the only people who got a password were those in our synergy database. Of course, we didn't just advise them of the new intranet's debut, we created a beautiful tri-fold, full color invitation with the big cheese, Mickey Mouse, pointing out the informational highlights available to each user. Individual invitations also included a password unique to each invitee.

The website served as an "exclusive" information resource. In addition to posting a list of all business units and the mission statements of each division, we created a searchable synergy directory with all database names, emails, fax numbers, etc., to make contact information readily available to all.

Users could also view upcoming film release schedules, lists of network and syndicated TV series under the Disney banner, Home Video releases, Consumer Products licensing programs, Publishing's catalog, ad rates for Disney magazines, sports game calendars, theme park special event schedules, and more.

Information on the site also included a list of ongoing "Synergy Opportunities". This was a comprehensive guide to existing company venues that could be used for marketing purposes such as poster locations in the theme parks, internal newsletters that could run stories about a given project, promotional message imprinting on company paycheck envelopes, and an overview of the process that enabled divisions to insert marketing messages in various video loops that ran in different Disney outlets such as the Disney Stores.

That loop, which was updated quarterly, was silent, only utilizing captions, but it offered business units the potential of reaching millions of consumers that visited the Disney Store annually.

Our print communications—Synergy News, Synergy This Month, Synergy Calendar, Corporate Priorities, Significant Disney Dates, Synergy FYI—moved online, too, and were archived there. Need-to-know synergy information was posted regularly, as well.

As soon as each new information piece was uploaded to Synergy Online, an automatic email was generated individually to each person in the database informing him or her of the "headline". The email also provided a simple click-through directly from their email message to the full informational piece on Synergy Online.

With the website, communication began to move even faster and could be more immediate. One example of when immediacy came into play was when the Broadway production of *Beauty and the Beast* opened in 1994. It was Disney's first New York stage production (based on the 1991 film of the same name), and everyone was anxious to hear about the reviews. The first thing in the morning after the New York opening, I posted a Synergy FYI online automatically triggering an email to our entire database. Following are excerpts from that communication:

"IT'S A HIT!"

On Tuesday, April 19, 1994, the Palace Theater broke the all-time Broadway box office record for a single day's ticket sales with *Disney's Beauty and the Beat: A New Musical*.

And last night, theatrical history had been made—and Disney entered a new field of family entertainment with its first Broadway stage production. The first-night audience responded with a standing ovation at the end of the performance with resounding cheers for this new visit with the cherished characters and beloved story of *Disney's Beauty and the Beast*.

The critics echoed the opening night audience's response to the production as well:

You will have the time of your life, your kids will have the time of their lives.

Joel Siegel
Good Morning America

The Magic Kingdom has come to Broadway ... the most eagerly awaited Broadway show in years, more than lives up to its advance build-up.

Ward Morehouse
Reuters

Beauty is exceptionally entertaining to watch—who can resist a talking teapot?—a merry, buoyant romp which should keep the Palace packed for decades. Not since *Peter Pan* has there been a better Broadway show for family outings with the small fry in tow.

Robert Osborne
The Hollywood Reporter

Not much can be added to the compliments that have been paid this magnificent new addition to the Disney legacy. Kudos and congratulations to the talented and dedicated team that made *Disney's Beauty and the Beast: The New Musical* Broadway's newest triumph.

The above was not only designed to inform, but also to motivate the synergy team to think about how they could coattail on the success of *Beauty and the Beast* on Broadway for their own divisions, thus expanding the scope of the entire project. Of course, we had the smartest and most creative (and probably only) synergy team in town, so this bit of stimulation was all that was needed to turn up the marketing heat on the stage version of *Beauty and the Beast*.

At the time Synergy Online was put into service, Cap Cities/ABC was still relatively new to The Walt Disney Company. Therefore, we took extra steps to bring them into the Synergy Online fold by partnering with Nancy DiBernardo, our key ABC synergy representative, to jointly present "Synergy Online Boot Camp Basic Training" to ABC marketing leaders at their corporate headquarters in New York City.

As was our Disney way for such special get-togethers, the request to participate was made by themed invitation. Using Army green as the predominant color and a stencil font for the headline, we developed an invitation with a fun military feel. It read:

> You have been chosen by the Disney Selective Service Committee to be drafted for active duty in Synergy Online Boot Camp
>
> Camp will be hosted by Disney Corporate Synergy and ABC Synergy. Here you will be armed with a private password and instructed on how to access and best utilize Disney's top-secret weapon—Synergy Online. You will also be privy to new intelligence information on upcoming and future developments to the system. Q&A will follow.

Acceptances poured in. DiBernardo handled the ABC side and we conducted a number of Synergy Online instructional sessions in what turned out to be a very successful boot camp event. To keep synergy top-of-mind after the fact, and keep everything in theme, we created Synergy Online dog tags that were presented to each ABC attendee. Our hope was that the site would serve as the perfect easy-to-use informational resource to bring ABC further into the synergy fold.

Although our synergy plates were really full, we continued to not only push the synergy envelope from a business standpoint, but promote our "brand" internally as well. Swag, like the Synergy Online dog tags, were important to our cause, too.

Early on when I sent out the Corporate Synergy Information Kit out to our database, it included a Disney Synergy logo button. Later came a host of items created exclusively for our synergy committee partners.

Over the years, Disney Synergy-branded wristwatches, baseball caps, t-shirts, briefcases, tote bags, and personal planners and organizers were gifted to the members of the group to invoke a sense of pride in their role as a synergy partner.

As we moved into the latter part of the 1990s, yet another important player joined the synergy team when Disney expanded its sports base taking control of a Major League baseball team, the California Angels.

The team's founder, entertainer Gene Autry, had owned the franchise for its first 36 years. When Disney took control, it extensively renovated the team's home base, Anaheim Stadium, that was then renamed Edison International Field of Anaheim. The team was also renamed the Anaheim Angels and became a subsidiary of a newly created Disney business unit called Disney Sports, Inc. (later renamed Anaheim Sports, Inc.). We welcomed yet another new synergy committee member to our ranks.

The last major new player on the Disney synergy field during my tenure at the company came with the announcement of a new business segment called Disney Cruise Line. It was founded in 1995 when Disney commissioned the building of two new ships. The *Disney Magic*, a state-of-the-art luxury cruiser, was the first ship launched and began sailing out of Port Canaveral, Florida, on July 30, 1998. On August 15, 1999, a sister ship, the *Disney Wonder*, took to the seas.

Jody Dreyer remembered a funny story about Michael Eisner and his first visit onboard the *Disney Magic*: "Michael was very inquisitive. We used to laugh because we'd be with him at some opening or something and we'd lose him. You'd turn around and he was gone."

In the case of Disney's first cruise ship, that's exactly what happened. "Somehow he had worked his way down to the ship's galley because he was so intrigued with how they did what they did on a cruise ship in often tight quarters. He was exploring like a little kid."

Both of Disney's family mega-cruisers were built by Europe's largest ship builder, Fincantieri, in Italy. They were sailed across the Atlantic to their home port in Florida. Disney Cruise Line and its new synergy representative joined the committee.

When Corporate Synergy began, who could imagine just how much The Walt Disney Company would grow and how important our function would become to the organization. We were an in-house communications agency with a full plate of "clients". The synergy function was expanded even further several years thereafter when synergy grew to become a global service.

A Synergy director, based at the Disney office in Paris, was appointed to handle Europe, and another, based at Disney in Hong Kong, to handle the Asia/Pacific region, and yet another was hired in Latin America to oversee that part of the world. All global reps occasionally attended our Burbank committee meetings, too. They all reported to Jody Dreyer. They also maintained an ongoing dialogue with my department providing us with all their communications that mirrored the same type of synergy program that had been developed at the studio. Synergy-wise, we were all in-sync even from a global perspective.

CHAPTER TWENTY-NINE

Results

All that I've written thus far has focused on how adding a synergy component to marketing plans can lead to phenomenally profitable results, not only for a company like Disney, but for any corporation that is willing to orchestrate it from the very top of the organization.

From my historical perspective, we scaled the top of the synergy hill on so many corporate priority projects. However, in my decade of work in this discipline, no project was as unbelievably synergy successful as the launch of the *The Lion King* on June 15, 1994. It seemed to take on a synergy life of its own as it blazed a pathway through every nook and cranny within the Disney organization.

Interestingly, when *The Lion King* first became an animation project, there wasn't much interest in it. According to Don Hahn, the film's director, "Nobody wanted to work on it. Everybody was gravitating to *Pocahontas* and I just couldn't get anyone interested. They'd say things like, "Who's going to want to see that?" But when we finally did get going, the whole synergy team was on it from about two years out and it certainly paid off for the company."

Needless to say, the synergy power driving that project over twenty years ago is still roaring strong today through the sale of thousands of consumer products including videos and DVDs played and replayed and replayed again through two generations of kids.

Communication, teamwork, and actively working something called synergy is most clearly exemplified by the profits that the company continues to derive from this property.

A few weeks after the movie opened I compiled a Synergy Recap Report, by business unit, for *The Lion King*. It included all the divisional cross-promotions in place on the day the film premiered. The compilation was massive (23 single-spaced typewritten pages) detailing hundreds of synergy partnerships promoting the film that swept its way through the entire Disney organization. The Disney business segments (as they existed under the Disney company umbrella in 1994) that participated in supporting *The Lion King* included:

Buena Vista Pictures Marketing, Buena Vista Pictures Distribution, Buena Vista International, Network TV Specials, Buena Vista Television, Buena Vista International TV/Buena Vista Productions, the Disney Channel, KCAL-TV (Disney-owned LA TV station), Buena Vista Home Video, Buena Vista International Home Video, Hollywood Records, Disney Licensing, Licensed Publishing, the Disney Store, Hyperion (Publishing), Disney Press, Mouse Works (Disney Publishing imprint), Disney Magazine Publishing, Walt Disney Art Classics, Walt Disney Records, Walt Disney Computer Software, Disney Collectibles, Disney Consumer Products, Disney Consumer Products International, Disneyland, Disneyland Hotel, Walt Disney World, Walt Disney World Resorts, Walt Disney Special Events Company, Attractions Merchandise, Magic Kingdom Club, Disney University, Walt Disney Imagineering, and Walt Disney World on Ice.

Adding to the hundreds of internal cross-promotions in place across the Disney landscape, even more national and local promotions were developed in conjunction with Disney Corporate Alliance partners and other major companies including Burger King, Nestle U.S.A., Delta Air Lines, Mattel Toys, General Foods, Payless Shoe Source, Kodak, AMC Theaters, and Skybox, among others. The sheer number of programs that supported *The Lion King* on opening day was eye-popping.

Ultimately, the film proved to be one of the all-time biggest box office winners in history. It also spawned *The Lion King on Broadway*, an enormously successful stage production that opened on November 13, 1997. It captured six Tony Awards including Best Musical.

To date, *The Lion King* has been running on the Great White Way for over twenty years and is still going strong along with productions running worldwide. Since its Broadway debut in 1997, the musical has been seen by an estimated 75 million people in 22 productions around the world and has grossed more than $6.2 billion, more than any other film or stage show in history.

The success of *The Lion King* is astonishing. And everybody mentioned in this book was a part of it. It blew the top off every Disney marketing benchmark that came before it.

Michael Eisner and Frank Wells were the synergy masters while the company marketers realized their vision. It was all based on working corporate "integration" as a team, as had been touted in *The Wall Street Journal* way back in 1958. Walt Disney would have been proud.

In fact, that team spirit was perhaps the most important thing I learned working at The Walt Disney Company in the Eisner and Wells era. It was fundamental to organizational success and permeated the culture whether in marketing or any other area of the company.

Jody Dreyer recalled, "I feel like the time we were all working together, it was just ready, set, go, and everybody was on the same page. We were all singing off the same song sheet."

Jack Lindquist remarked, "No matter what you did on an event, it was based on teamwork and you did your part. No one, no matter what level, ever said something like "I'm too big to do that." It didn't exist. And nobody would say "That's my idea or I'm taking credit for it." We just worked together and we never let any bumps in the road or disagreements take our eye off the ball."

Tim O'Day, former Disney PR executive, said, "How we all worked together reminds me of the old game Pickup Stix. You pull one stick out and everything falls apart. Our teams never fell apart. They may have changed through the course of realizing a project, but they never fell apart."

Former Walt Disney World marketing executive Phil Lengyel remembered one important factor that also added greatly to our success: "We did what we did because it came from our heart."

How lucky I was to have a career that I so enjoyed. It was like playing in a big sandbox with other kids who were having as much fun as me. Confucius said, "Choose a job you love, and you will never have to work a day in your life." I surely did.

Thank you to Walt Disney for creating such an amazing organization. And to Michael Eisner and Frank Wells who re-ignited the spark that elevated the company to unparalleled new heights. Kudos also go to those who continue to carry the success of The Walt Disney Company well into the 21st century.

To all the remarkable people with whom I had the privilege of working and who taught me so much about marketing, I treasure the time we spent together and love that so many of us continue to maintain valued friendships to this day.

What was it like being inside the Disney marketing machine? It was unforgettable.

Acknowledgments

During my twenty-two years at the Walt Disney Company I had the good fortune of meeting and working with so many great people. For this book, I interviewed a number of Disney colleagues that were key to illustrating what it was like to be inside the Disney marketing machine during the era of Michael Eisner and Frank Wells. Their firsthand stories, anecdotes, and memories, made this book possible.

In that regard, thank you to (in no particular order): Jack Lindquist, Phil Lengyel, Linda Warren, Jody Dreyer, Mike Davis, Dave Goodman, Arlene Ludwig, Michael Russell, Tim O'Day, Tony Baxter, Dave Lancashire, Marilyn Magness, Don Hahn, Charlie Ridgway, Tony Perri, Lindsay Schnebly, Cindy Spodek-Dickey, Jane Gordon, Jeff Hoffman, Anne White, Ron Kollen, Scott Brinegar, and Bob Witter. Special thanks to Michael Eisner and Frank Wells whose spoken words were shared via the many books and articles in which they talked about their Disney experiences.

Also a big thank you to Paula Sigman (formerly a Walt Disney Company Archives executive) for editing the book for Disney accuracy per company history, dates, nomenclature, etc. Thank you also to my buddy Tim O'Day for taking the time to read the manuscript and provide editing expertise as well.

And to Sam Tuchman, my first boss at NBC, thank you for writing the foreword. You were an outstanding role model for me so early in my working life. What I learned from you was professionalism with kindness, an attribute that impacted the rest of my career.

To my publisher, Bob McLain, at Theme Park Press, thank you for believing in my book concept and giving me the thumbs-up to move forward. It's been a joy to relive the memories.

About the Author

Lorraine Santoli, former director of Corporate Synergy for The Walt Disney Company, has established herself as an innovative communicator, creative thinker, writer, and idea specialist.

Santoli began her career in the entertainment business at the NBC Television Network in New York City, where she honed her business and creative skills in TV and radio research as well as becoming one of NBC's first female camera operators. After nearly ten years with NBC, in 1978 Santoli left broadcasting and relocated to the West Coast where she joined the Walt Disney Company.

Over a 22-year Disney career, Santoli worked her way up the Disney organization from marketing assistant to TV and motion picture publicist, to Supervisor of Publicity at Disneyland, to manager, and finally director of Corporate Synergy for entire the Walt Disney Company under the leadership of Michael Eisner and Frank Wells. In that pivotal role she coordinated all internal cross-promotions for over 50 diverse Disney businesses—from Film and Television to Home Entertainment, Consumer Products, Sports, Theatrical Productions, and Theme Parks.

Today, Santoli resides in New York's Westchester county and is an accomplished freelance writer, book author, journalist, and speaker. She also served as executive director of the Annette Funicello Research Fund for Neurological Diseases from 2010–2013.

Contact Lorraine Santoli through her website, SantoliCommunications. com, or by email: marketingmachine@icloud.com.

About the Publisher

Theme Park Press is the largest independent publisher of Disney and Disney-related pop culture books in the world.

Established in November 2012 by Bob McLain, Theme Park Press has released best-selling print and digital books about such topics as Disney films and animation, the Disney theme parks, Disney historical and cultural studies, park touring guides, autobiographies, fiction, and more.

Theme Park Press authors and contributors are a Disney who's who, ranging from well-known Disney historians and commentators like Jim Korkis, Sam Gennawey, and Didier Ghez, to Disney notables and legends like Floyd Norman, Bill "Sully" Sullivan, Rolly Crump, and Bob Gurr.

For our complete catalog and a list of forthcoming titles, please visit:

ThemeParkPress.com

or contact the publisher at:

bob@themeparkpress.com

. . . .

Theme Park Press Newsletter

For a free, occasional email newsletter to keep you posted on new book releases, new author signings, and other events, as well as contests and exclusive excerpts and supplemental content, send email to:

theband@themeparkpress.com

or sign up at

ThemeParkPress.com

. . . .

More Books from Theme Park Press

Theme Park Press publishes dozens of books each year for Disney fans and for general and academic audiences. Here are just a few of our titles. For the complete catalog, including book descriptions and excerpts, please visit:

ThemeParkPress.com

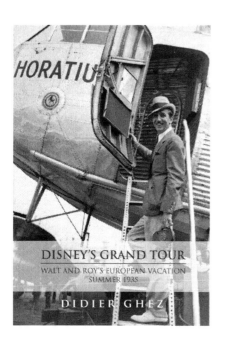

DISNEY'S GRAND TOUR
WALT AND ROY'S EUROPEAN VACATION
SUMMER 1935

DIDIER GHEZ

THE
RIDE DELEGATE
Memoir of a Walt Disney World VIP Tour Guide

Annie Salisbury

Brittany
EARNS
HER EARS

My Secret Walt Disney World
Cast Member Diary

BRITTANY DICOLOGERO
Earning Your Ears: Volume Five

Great Big
Beautiful
Tomorrow

Walt Disney
and Technology

Christian Moran
with Rolly Crump,
Bob Gurr, Jim Korkis,
Sam Gennawey and Dr.
Maureen Furniss, PhD

A Historical Tour of
Walt Disney World

Jungle Cruise · Pirates of the Caribbean · Enchanted Tiki Room · Crystal Palace · Main Street, U.S.A. · Carousel of Progress · Tomorrowland

VOLUME I

ANDREW KISTE

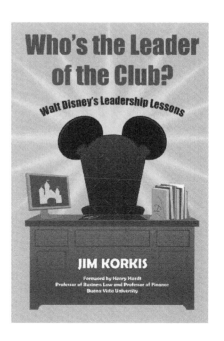

Who's the Leader of the Club?

Walt Disney's Leadership Lessons

JIM KORKIS

Foreword by Henry Hardt
Professor of Business Law and Professor of Finance
Buena Vista University

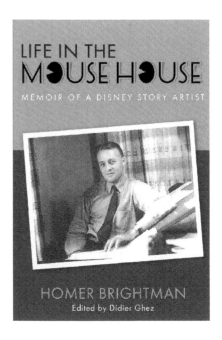

LIFE IN THE
M♥USE H♥USE

MEMOIR OF A DISNEY STORY ARTIST

HOMER BRIGHTMAN
Edited by Didier Ghez

MOUSE IN TRANSITION

An Insider's Look at
Disney Feature Animation

STEVE HULETT
Foreword by John Musker
Disney Feature Films Animation Director

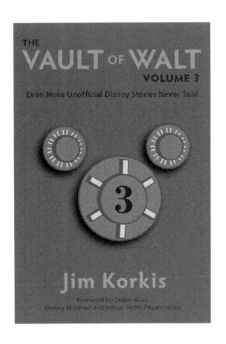

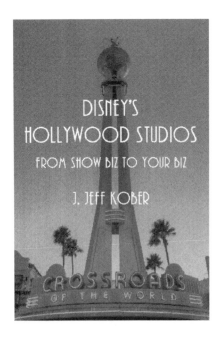

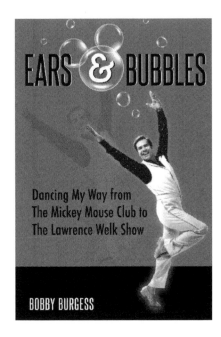

27829309R00103

Printed in Great Britain
by Amazon